D1495588

PRAISE FOR *BUSINESS INSIDE OUT*

"This book is like 'Gay Marketing 101.' It is required reading for anyone learning about the gay and lesbian consumer market and written by some of the best pros in the business."
MICHAEL WILKE, FOUNDING EXECUTIVE DIRECTOR, COMMERCIAL CLOSET ASSOCIATION

*"*Business Inside Out *makes a compelling case for not just why but how to include GLBT customers and employees in your organization's marketing and policy actions. Bob Witeck and Wes Combs have literally written the book on successful marketing to this emerging market segment."*
TIM KINCAID, MANAGER, CORPORATE COMMUNICATIONS, AMERICAN AIRLINES

"The GLBT community, with its significant buying power and strong influential ability, is a market that every consumer business should not only pay attention to but also understand. Business Inside Out *will help you understand this market. Using real-life examples, Bob Witeck and Wes Combs speak the language of marketing, media, brand value, and customer loyalty–supported by a strong market research foundation. I suggest you read it before your competition does."*
GREGORY T. NOVAK, PRESIDENT AND CEO, HARRIS INTERACTIVE INC.

"This book is a must-read for anyone who wants to understand why the GLBT consumer is one of the most valuable and loyal niche demographics for advertisers and marketers."
LISA SHERMAN, GENERAL MANAGER AND SENIOR VICE PRESIDENT, MTV NETWORKS' LOGO

*"*Business Inside Out *offers fundamental insights for today's GLBT business community and the GLBT consumer. If you're looking for a definitive resource with real-world experiences, you'll find it from Bob Witeck and Wes Combs–true experts in marketing and savvy business."*
SELISSE BERRY, EXECUTIVE DIRECTOR, OUT & EQUAL WORKPLACE ADVOCATES

"Corporate leadership today means leaving no GLBT employee, customer, or shareholder behind. We're lucky that two of the forces behind this momentum are found in Bob Witeck and Wes Combs, and

in their book, Business Inside Out, *which translates their seasoned smarts into action for all business leaders."*
JOE SOLMONESE, PRESIDENT, HUMAN RIGHTS CAMPAIGN

"Bob Witeck and Wes Combs practically invented the science of marketing to the lesbian and gay community. Business Inside Out *is a great resource that combines social equality with savvy business practices."*
GARY J. GATES, COAUTHOR OF *THE GAY AND LESBIAN ATLAS*

"Bob Witeck and Wes Combs are the foremost experts in the U.S. on the buying habits of gay Americans. They teach what many major companies are learning: gay and lesbian consumers are loyal to companies that are loyal to them."
ELIZABETH BIRCH, CEO, KIDRO PRODUCTIONS, INC.

Best! Bob Witeck 10-05-06

Dear Mike and Tony — thanks for your support!

ROBERT WITECK | **WESLEY COMBS**

Business Inside Out

CAPTURING MILLIONS OF BRAND LOYAL GAY CONSUMERS

KAPLAN) PUBLISHING

This publication is designed to provide accurate and authoritative information in regard to the subject matter covered. It is sold with the understanding that the publisher is not engaged in rendering legal, accounting, or other professional service. If legal advice or other expert assistance is required, the services of a competent professional should be sought.

President, Kaplan Publishing: Roy Lipner
Vice President and Publisher: Maureen McMahon
Senior Acquisitions Editor: Michael Cunningham
Senior Managing Editor, Production: Jack Kiburz
Typesetter: the dotted i
Cover Designer: Design Solutions

Published by Kaplan Publishing,
a division of Kaplan, Inc.

Printed in the United States of America

06 07 08 10 9 8 7 6 5 4 3 2 1

Library of Congress Cataloging-in-Publication Data

Witeck, Robert.
  Business inside out : capturing millions of brand-loyal gay consumers /
Robert Witeck and Wesley Combs.
      p. cm.
  Includes index.
  ISBN-13: 978-1-4195-0520-1
  ISBN-10: 1-4195-0520-3
  1. Gay consumers—United States. 2. Target marketing—United States.
I. Combs, Wesley. II. Title.
  HF5415.33.U6W58 2006
  658.80086'640973—dc22

                                                              2006015551

Contents

Foreword

As a young man first starting out on the corporate ladder, privileged with Harvard and Michigan degrees, there were many things I was sure that I knew. A solid education and self-confidence are gifts almost any American might envy.

Yet, looking back today, there were at least two important things I did not know. I did not yet know I was gay, nor could any of us then have possibly known what extraordinary and valuable leaps gays and lesbians would make in changing corporate America over the years.

Throughout my long career, I always understood that first things come first in business and that meant keeping my focus on my work. When I acknowledged to many that I remained unattached, it was easy to add truthfully that I was married to my job. I am personally humbled by and grateful for the shared successes I found throughout my rewarding professional roles at Ford Motor Company. I often feel I have been one of the luckiest people in corporate America.

My personal life, however, was a silent chapter—at best a distraction to me and a secret from others. Over time, of course, I learned that honestly being myself was a plus and not a weakness.

Consider that when I began my career in the 1960s, advancement and management appointments were all but impossible for even well-qualified women and racial minorities. What possible chance then was there for professional success and acceptance for an openly gay man?

There's no question the corporate closet remains even today. Yet the marketplace and the workplace are accelerating the unmistakable and favorable trends of acceptance and inclusion of all. That is the real business story that Bob Witeck and Wes Combs tell persuasively about the gay market in *Business Inside Out,* and they echo my own day-to-day experiences navigating through boardrooms, factory floors, and showrooms.

Today successful corporate leaders are pragmatists as well as fierce competitors. They recognize that diversity is not simply the right thing to do. It is also the smart thing to do, as they have learned the best talent and loyal customers cannot be found in a single look-alike group. Profitability for any company worth its salt is based on two things—really knowing your customers and recruiting and retaining the best talent possible.

Gays, lesbians, bisexuals, and transgender people, like their counterparts, have worked hard and persevered in business. The difference today is that so many more of us are valued and visible, successful and welcomed, along with our relationships, families, and spending power. In the economic realm, we are counted among executives, managers, workers, board members, investors, entrepreneurs, and, of course, consumers.

A business leader can decide to follow his or her own personal beliefs, but successful organizations will select pluralism and diversity as an essential part of their DNA. Some companies will want to be leaders in eliminating homophobia and in providing fully equal treatment for gays and lesbians. The last acceptable prejudice is one too many. Yes, companies are in business to succeed and prosper, but discrimination and intolerance are never good business.

As you pick up this first-of-its-kind book, you will learn much about the newest trends and opportunities in this evolving market. Grounded in state-of-the-art research and a trusted, seasoned eye, *Business Inside Out* not only describes the emerging gay marketplace and workplace but also offers down-to-earth tips and expert resources that guide companies and organizations to understand, act, and communicate confidently in this refreshing, new arena.

Allan Gilmour, former Vice Chairman, Ford Motor Company

Acknowledgments

Our acknowledgments are many, both professional and, more often, very personal. We sincerely wish to honor all of them here.

As marketers, we identify most with socially responsible companies and causes that equally prize values-based communications. While blazing trails and building bridges within the gay market, our professional roles also have specialized in responding to urgent social and health issues, such as HIV/AIDS, women's health, disability barriers, and surviving with cancer. In this arena, we were privileged to work with Michael Manganiello and to represent the late Christopher Reeve and Dana Reeve, whose examples and sheer intellects educated millions about the power of medical research to cure spinal paralysis one day as well as care for the millions living with paralysis. How could we not be inspired by these two extraordinary individuals!

We learn every day from our gifted and dedicated colleagues, who use these lessons in our work with Witeck-Combs clients. We thank each of them (as well as our former staffers) every single day, not only for their friendship but also for making our work possible and our clients successful every day: John Butler, Colleen Dermody, Alyssa Friedland, Shameka Lloyd, Roberto Munoz, Michael Vallebuona, and Robertine Watson. We thank our clients above all for their steadfast partnership, and especially for giving us the chance year in and year out to craft successful strategies on their behalf.

Our skills are richly enhanced by many colleagues and leaders in their own fields. Their expert contributions are beyond counting, and they often point our way to truly original thinking. We are especially indebted to our partners at Harris Interactive for believing in our mission and letting us share in theirs: David Krane, Bryan Krulikowski, Greg Novak, Jim Quilty, Judy Ricker, Humphrey Taylor, Scott Upham, Nancy Wong, and John Bremer stand out, along with many more of their talented bench.

In academia, we acknowledge with profound gratitude the teamwork and contributions of several notable scholars and very gifted writers, particularly Lee Badgett, John Burnett, John D'Emilio, Gary Gates, Larry Gross, Greg Herek, Caitlin Ryan, Katherine Sender, Ken Sherrill, Rodger Streitmatter, and Tracy Ryan. They have taught us so much for so long, and we celebrate their accomplishments in furthering social science and enlightenment on gay and lesbian issues.

When we began our work in 1993, gay, lesbian, bisexual, and transgender (GLBT) equality in the workplace and opportunities in the marketplace were in their earliest stages. We have been so fortunate to work alongside some of the most visionary GLBT business leaders and their straight allies in corporate America who have been true pioneers. We must single out our first client, American Airlines, and our friends Robbin Burr, George Carrancho, Rick Cirillo, David Currier, Michael Fricke, Wes Friedman, Roger Frizzell, Katya Hazel, Robert Hosey, Debra Hunter-Johnson, Tim Kincaid, Mary Sanderson, Rick Wilbins, and Betty Young. As a former IBM employee, Wes was especially grateful to work with Joseph Bertolotti, Yvette Burton, Mike Fuller, and Sarah Siegel, who have set the highest standard for other companies to follow. At Ford Motor Company, former VP of global marketing Jan Valentic had the foresight to understand the value of GLBT consumers to the world's largest automaker. Her groundbreaking analysis was carried on by these current executives at Ford Volvo, Jaguar, and Land Rover, including Sally Eastwood, Connie Fontaine, Heather Harkovich, John Maloney, Sylvia Lopez Navarro, and Susan Pepper, as well as former executives Dai Min Barclay, Lynn Bonner, Karina Jaramillo-Saa, and Craig Stacey. We would be deeply remiss, too, if we failed to thank our friend, mentor, and Ford's former chief financial officer and executive, Allan Gilmour.

The breadth and visibility of the GLBT consumer market allowed for the emergence in mid-2005 of Logo, MTV Networks' advertising-supported gay and lesbian cable network. We feel honored to work alongside the latest pioneers in this marketplace, including David Bittler, Lori Chee, Nakiah Cherry-Chinchilla, Deena Demasi, Carter Etherington, Matt Farber, Kristin Frank, Brian Graden, Karen Habib, Jessica Heacock, Juan Herrera, Jamie Ideue, Joanne Jacobson, Michael Lanzilotta, Marc Leonard, Judy McGrath, Carole Robinson, Jon Sechrist, Lisa Sherman, Jeanine Smartt, Carole Smith, Eileen Opatut, Chris Wagley, and Tom Watson.

At Motorola, we are proud also to acknowledge our colleagues and champions, including Omar Albertelli, Marjorie Chorlins, Kathleen Finato, Stephanie Turner, and Bob Williams.

We also gladly credit many of our nonprofit colleagues for their expert contributions to the gay marketplace as well as their tireless work as change agents for fairness and equal treatment in the workplace: Jill Eynon, Candace Gingrich, Daryl Herrschaft, John Lake, Samir Luther, Jeff Mack, Barbara Menard, Cathy Nelson, Mark Shields, David Smith, Jay Smith, and Christopher Speron at the Human Rights Campaign; Selisse Berry, Dave Bueche, and Dan Tussey at Out & Equal Workplace Advocates; Malcolm Lazin at the Equality Forum; Chance Mitchell and Justin Nelson at the National Gay & Lesbian Chamber of Commerce; and Mike Wilke at the Commercial Closet Association.

Many of our fellow professionals have helped pioneer the growth and development of the gay market, opening new business opportunities and earning professional accolades. Among many talented peers whose many contributions and achievements we value, we wish to thank Cindy Abel, Nancy Becker, Tim Bennett, Stephanie Blackwood, Mike Borschow, Howard Buford, Sean Bugg, Margaret Conway, Pam Derderian, Judy Dlugacz,

Mark Elderkin, Amy Errett, Todd Evans, Ben Finzel, Margot Friedman, Susan Gore, John Graves, Jeff Guaracino, Gregg Kaminsky, Michael Lamb, Joe Landry, Gregg Lieberman, Dennis Lonergan, Fran Marranca, Brian McNaught, John McMullen, Dawn Meifert, Andrew Mersmann, Sally Michael, Robert Moore, John Nash, Kelli O'Donnell, Mike Phelps, J.R. Pratts, Robert Raben, Cathy Renna, Tom Roth, Charlie Rounds, Ed Salvato, Sivan Schlecter, Walter Schubert, Lowell Selvin, Randy Shulman, Scott Seitz, Matt Skallerud, Scott Swenson, Don Tuthill, Joe Valentino, Judy Wieder, and Liz Winfeld. Through innovative advertising and marketing, events promotion, corporate counsel, and media mastery, many of these professionals have made a difference to the gay community through their expertise and dedication. We are very grateful to the thoughtful intellects and passion of commentators like Paul Varnell and Stephen Hunt. Through their stewardship of the National Lesbian & Gay Journalists Association and commitment to excellence in journalism, we also are very grateful to Robert Dodge, Eric Hegedus, Steven Petrow, and Pamela Strother. We are especially honored to salute the legacy of journalist and NLGJA founder, the late Leroy Aarons.

We feel blessed with friendships, support for, and allegiance to many gifted civil rights advocates, spokespersons, and community leaders. We especially honor John Aravosis, Tammy Baldwin, Mickie Ballotta, Vic Basile, Terry Bean, Aaron Belkin, Michelle Benecke, Elizabeth Birch, David Bohnett, Craig Bowman, Keith Boykin, Bruce Brothers, Rea Carey, David Catania, Kevin Cathcart, Ken Cheuvront, Jerry Clark, Kecia Cunningham, Dick Dadey, Kathleen DeBold, Betty DeGeneres, Adam Ebbin, Steve Elmendorf, Jay Fisette, Michael Fleming, Matt Foreman, Charles Francis, Barney Frank, Robert Gant, Joan Garry, Ethan Geto, Tim Gill, Neil Giuliano, Jim Graham, Patrick Guerriero, Steve Gunderson, Herb Hamsher, Steve Herbits, Donald Hitchcock, Jody Huckaby, Lori Jean, Kevin Jennings, Chad Johnson, Emily Jones, Frank Kameny, Kate Kendall, Jim Kolbe, Judith Light, Renee Lohman, Deacon Maccubbin, Rodger McFarlane, Tim McFeeley, Kris McLaughlin, David Mixner, Anne

Nenneau, David Noble, Torie Osborn, Dixon Osburn, Libby Post, Julian Potter, Jonathan Rauch, Donna Redwing, Sheila Reid-Alexander, Gina Reiss, Alexander Robinson, Mike Rogers, Bob Rosen, Hilary Rosen, Rick Rosendall, Jim Roth, Mirian Saez, Andrea Sharrin, Craig Shniderman, Paul Smedberg, Nadine Smith, Mary Snider, Joe Solmonese, Winnie Stachelberg, B.J. Stiles, John Tanzella, Andy Tobias, Jeff Trammell, Urvashi Vaid, Rikki Wilchins, Chris Wolf, Chuck Wolfe, Evan Wolfson, Cathy Woolard, Paul Yandura, and Daniel Zingale, each of whom unselfishly has given leadership, passion, and voice to our aspiring community.

The friends who believed in us all of these years, we regret, are far too numerous to name one by one. And with our families who love us unconditionally, you each give us constant purpose and strength for which we can never repay our debt.

Our partners, Bob Connelly and Greg Albright, have given us each the greatest inspiration of all. Without you in our lives, nothing is possible.

Bob Witeck and Wes Combs

Introduction

What inspires you?

Inspiration to us is a powerful human feeling. It can help us each move mountains, create innovations, cure diseases, or change minds. It is the intangible energy that drives an individual, a business, or an organization to succeed. As professional communicators and business owners, and as human beings, we always are seekers of inspiration. In time, we hope to inspire others.

The lessons we have learned over the last decade and a half of work in the gay consumer market continue to inspire us today. They enable us to pursue new industries and challenges, break down mindless outdated barriers, and shatter stereotypes, myths, and meanness that keep people from understanding the true breadth, depth, and values of America's gay community.

We wrote this book in part because of the generous inspiration we have received from others, and our strong desire to share much of this valuable experience. As openly gay professionals, we also hope to turn "business inside out" to understand, describe, and celebrate the many hidden yet essential contributions gay men, lesbians, bisexual men and women, and transgender people (GLBT) make to America's economy and to our public life. Perhaps this will help inspire corporate America to build more bridges with gay America, for many more GLBT people to aspire to be all they can be, and for gay entrepreneurs to realize their own dreams.

This book is intended for many kinds of readers. We have written it to speak directly to marketers who worry their competitors may be beating them to the punch in reaching gay households. Experts in market research will absorb and consider key findings about gay consumer behaviors. Advertisers and media planners will benefit from learning many of the latest insights about gay media consumption and brand loyalty. Executives will also appreciate the enduring resonance of corporate reputation, and communicators will consider effective strategies for recognizing, managing, and coping with cultural backlash.

For all readers, we hope they will find this as truthful as it is helpful in dispelling myth and stereotype in understanding GLBT households and marketplace. All of these fundamentals spring from our experience within corporate America. They are lessons renewed from working day to day with real clients, colleagues, and co-workers who respond to real marketing opportunities, real problems, and real pressures.

The lessons also come from our day-to-day experience as leaders in the gay community. We learned long ago that reliable market research, business experience, and accurate knowledge are key to building a profitable case for the gay consumer market. Decision makers would never be moved merely by anecdotes, intuition, or hunches alone—we had to speak the same language.

Our company has a unique approach with our own expert strengths, we think. It is a marketing communications and public relations agency that develops and implements comprehensive communications strategies that help an organization effectively reach the GLBT audience.

We find that corporations hoping to build bridges with the gay marketplace must bring together many disciplines from market research, advertising, direct marketing, employee communications, public affairs, community relationships, and all forms of earned and paid media, as well as critical thinking about message and crisis planning.

We also understand that today's nonprofit organizations need to understand how best to communicate their issues both to GLBT and mainstream audiences. Today, GLBT issues impact public, school, and workplace policies, as well as media and entertainment images. Our role is to help these organizations clearly communicate to their members and the general public how these issues impact their daily lives.

Almost as important as what we do and how we do our work is what our company is not. It is not a market research firm, though we invest significantly in developing and finding the best possible consumer research available. It is not an advertising agency, though we ally ourselves with outstanding creative partners and agencies to achieve top results.

Putting all of these pieces together makes perfect sense to us, and allows us to offer a 360-degree perspective. That is the perspective we have tried to bring sensibly to this book too.

The trends we are seeing in business today are encouraging and exciting. When we began our work almost 14 years ago, developing a targeted campaign or a communications strategy to connect with gay households was not entirely new ground. Many, many others have paved the way and opened doors in corporate America to fresh thinking and new opportunities.

However, at that time it was still refreshing and bold for companies to expand their policies of inclusion, and adventurous for marketers to dedicate budgets to reaching and including GLBT homes and neighborhoods. Within the next decade, of course, we predict sea changes even bolder and more adventurous. We recognize that equal workplace policies and same-sex partner benefits for GLBT employees will become nearly commonplace, and that advances in market and demographic research will propel a wider range of strategies that include same-sex couples and households in almost all market sectors. Knowledge emboldens business action.

This book is a road map that will help marketing professionals and business communicators navigate their future journey too. We hope you can apply much of this practical experience, the latest research, and case studies to opening up economic bridges to gay households throughout America. To help do so, we have divided our book into three parts.

Part One, called "The Background," consists of four chapters in which we discuss the history of the gay marketplace and media—to underscore the path of gays, lesbians, bisexuals, and transgender people from stigma to visibility.

This rich context and background will make what follows more understandable and applicable. We insert a mix of history, including our own, to show where and how we actually began. We start by trying to dispel myths up front, such as the unsupported expectation that all gay consumers are pretty much alike, or that they presumably all reflect the tastes and wallet of an upscale, gay, white urban male. We will try to underscore the rich complexity and nature of gay households so there is more awareness of the things that make us different from other households, as well as what makes us the same as many others.

Part Two digs deeper into consumer identity, demographics, and behaviors; in short, the actual metrics and understanding about GLBT consumers that smart marketers will need to grasp. We describe the nature and meaning of buying power, differences and similarities in buying attitudes, brand loyalty, and other concepts that so often are associated with the gay consumer market. We call this section "The Opportunity," and you will see why.

Part Three offers readers our very best tips and practical examples that help guide our clients and other corporations and organizations in achieving their objectives. In this section, we illustrate "The Strategy" that overarches a campaign, and apply the knowledge and understanding picked up earlier. We are very proud to illustrate our story with behind-the-scenes details about a precedent-setting campaign we launched with a popular automobile brand that earned the industry's very first recognition for a popular gay-friendly marketing strategy.

In addition, we highlight in our final chapter the seasoned counsel necessary for companies to understand the nature and the implications of cultural backlash. We aim to ensure they feel confident responding to customer anxieties or to critics effectively while maintaining their primary focus on business objectives. In Part Three, we also provide expert resources, organizations, and allies who also partner with companies and institutions to assist them in their objectives and enrich their knowledge about the diverse GLBT community.

PART ONE

The Background

CHAPTER 1

Why Reputation Really Matters

When we first imagined launching our own marketing communications and public relations firm over a dozen years ago, we asked ourselves many practical and many ambitious questions.

Where will we find clients? What services can we offer? Where should we open our doors? What will it take to succeed apart from a hope and a prayer and hard work?

More important, however, we quickly realized there was one critical question we absolutely needed to answer for ourselves. Exactly what kind of a public relations and marketing communications company would we be? How would we be known?

In any major American city, and especially in Washington, D.C., we know there are countless public relations firms and marketing consultants. The knowledge, skills, and practice of communications take many forms. Well-qualified professionals abound who advise companies, associations, and nonprofits on marketing strategies, and who also write news releases, speeches, commercial scripts, online blogs, marketing brochures, you name it. There are global companies and one-person practices and everything in between.

What, we wondered, might make us truly stand out? What would be our competitive edge? Good questions. We discovered the right answers in our identity as openly gay professionals.

In the early 1990s, as gay men and as friends and colleagues, we witnessed extraordinary progress, along with confusion, risk, and peril in the ways that corporate America understood the gay, lesbian, bisexual, and transgender (GLBT) community. We saw that gay identity was truly emerging in many forms of popular culture, on television, and in American political life, and beginning to create hints and opportunities in our marketplace—mostly hints and just a few early opportunities.

As volunteers for GLBT civil rights causes and AIDS benefits, we brought much-needed professional expertise to these fledgling organizations that, at the time, did not have the resources to hire help themselves. While this was personally fulfilling, we saw a disturbing disconnect between the gay community and the professional world in which we had worked for many years.

Corporations had high standards and metrics for compliance when establishing partnerships with nonprofits, a new territory for most organizations. The issues these nonprofits addressed created new challenges to corporations that were suddenly being judged by the GLBT company they were keeping. Wherever we turned, we saw stunning examples of ignorance, stereotypes, stigma, myths, and a few glimmers of light and acceptance in the business arena.

GAY ISSUES AND AMERICAN LIFE: THEN AND NOW

Remember America in 1993. At that time, relatively few U.S. companies posted written nondiscrimination guidelines in their employment policies and practices that included sexual orientation. Almost none offered equal workplace benefits to the same-sex partners of their employees. And, policies protecting employees on the basis of gender identity and expression were nonexistent.

Throughout the United States, corporate America seemed to maintain a wall of self-imposed ignorance and indifference at best. At worst, it allowed shameful examples of job discrimination, management-sanctioned bigotry, and glass ceilings in promotion practices when it came to the capable and determined gay and lesbian employees in their midst. For the occasional transgender employee, and for brave individuals who self-identified as bisexual, the climate appeared to be completely opaque or hostile.

At that time, in almost the entire United States and in most jurisdictions, it was perfectly lawful for employers to fire men and women for being gay, lesbian, bisexual, or transgender. [As we write this today, 17 states, the District of Columbia, and numerous cities and municipalities have enacted nondiscrimination statutes, but sadly, it is still legal in most states in America to openly discriminate against lesbians and gays in the workplace.] Even with this slow progress, corporate America was helping to lead the way for state and local legislatures to enact the same protections for their citizens.

True, in the beginning of the 1990s there were oases of workplace responsibility and selective business leadership. The high-tech industry recognized early that what made one company more successful than another were the skills and the quality of their employees. To be the most competitive firm out there, each and every employee had potential value to a company's bottom line. Corporate leaders like Lotus and IBM (which later acquired Lotus) were quick to understand that adding sexual orientation nondiscrimination policies sent a loud signal to GLBT employees that they were welcome.

Soon, other companies began to take other tentative steps, such as sanctioning gay employee resource groups and putting them on a par with other loyal employee groups. The much-stretched and sometimes misunderstood word *diversity*—describing African-American, Hispanic, Asian, and female workers at the time—was beginning to take on new meaning to include other categories of workers, particularly open, honest, and self-identified gays and lesbians.

From our optimistic perspective, we envisioned a world where gays and lesbians were fully visible and valued. While full-muscled advocates for fairness and social policy improvements, we also are realists and we understand the actual pace of progress. We know that electoral and legislative reform to achieve civil rights can and often does take generations. Consider the often-incremental progress made toward African-American civil rights, the equal treatment and standing of women in society, and the uneven improvements made by people with disability.

While each civil rights movement has its own history and its own ethos, all such movements have common threads. We knew that achieving our goals would not happen in only one arena or simply be won one day at the ballot box. We believed that commerce and business ought to take leading roles too, and address the inequities and invisibility of gays and lesbians in many more ways.

More important, based on our firsthand experience, we knew that the marketplace is dynamic and competitive while also being reactive. Smart business leaders and entrepreneurs were likely to sense and respond to trends if they also advanced their business objectives. If civil rights progress and full inclusion were accompanied by measurable economic benefits, then the marketplace will win too. How could it not?

Entrepreneurs tend to be passionate individuals. We had an unshakeable passion to be authentic and trusted communicators and to build our business on the universal values of respect and acceptance. How else would we realize the unlimited potential for all gays and lesbians to achieve their own success? The market was our stage, and the language of business was our script.

We also had firsthand experience of what it was like to be gay in corporate America. Wes worked for IBM from 1985 until 1992 at a time when gay issues were not yet at the forefront of the company's now-very-well-established, gay-friendly reputation. Bob worked on Capitol Hill and then for the public relations giant Hill & Knowlton. We understood differences in treatment and inclusion, and yet realized how as white male professionals, we could "pass" as heterosexual in the straight male dominant culture of our time.

Recognizing inequality in many forms just drove us to spend much of our spare time working with GLBT civil rights groups like the Human Rights Campaign to support policy changes and help elect gay-friendly legislators who could expand the definition of equality to include gay Americans. Finally, we realized that our daytime jobs just did not allow us to be the complete employees we wanted to be. We were devoting all of our energy to our jobs instead of worrying about who knew we were gay and whether that would hold us back in our career advances. Those are modest challenges, perhaps, considering other and more hurtful forms of antigay discrimination; yet enough to challenge us to rethink our future as professionals.

It was in pursuit of this dream that we founded our company.

To save money like any modest start-up enterprise, we simply put our desks together in Wes's basement along with our computers, phone lines, and file cabinets. Fortunately, as a time-saver, we could also wash and dry our laundry in the next room. We were expert multitaskers.

Two remarkable moments occurred in those first few weeks after we opened our business and embarked on our original mission: the chance to promote National Coming Out Day and the opportunity to help American Airlines shape its policies.

National Coming Out Day as a Communications Launch Pad

We first were given the special opportunity to shape and promote National Coming Out Day as an educational project of the Human Rights Campaign Fund. [Today, the Human Rights Campaign Fund, of course, is simply the Human Rights Campaign (www.hrc.org). The Human Rights Campaign, founded over 25 years ago, is the nation's largest civil rights advocacy group working for GLBT equality. With nearly a million members, donors, allies, and supporters, its work reaches communities, campuses, workplaces, and families all over America.]

Just a few years earlier, the late activist and educator Jean O'Leary and Rob Eichberg, with several allies, conceived the idea of a day each year to celebrate gay visibility, honesty, and acceptance. Eichberg, O'Leary, and others believed that the fastest way to get Americans to accept gays and lesbians was by knowing them. So, it was critical for members of the gay community to be open and honest with their friends, family members, and co-workers. It was simply about changing hearts and minds one person at a time, if necessary.

It was equally important to support individuals who were afraid merely to say who they really are and seek unconditional acceptance from family, friends, and co-workers. The concept was intended to benefit people of all ages who are anxious about being open and honest as GLBT people, but younger people who were beginning their adult journeys quickly embraced it. National Coming Out Day was marked annually for October 11 to commemorate the anniversary of the 1987 March on Washington for gay equality.

At that time, the gifted artist Keith Haring crafted a very simple, unforgettable line rendering of a human figure coming out of the proverbial closet. The Haring illustration represented the emergence of an openly gay person. The popular image quickly became closely identified as National Coming Out Day's symbol and message.

In 1993, Eichberg realized another dream by merging this important mission with the Human Rights Campaign, ensuring that National Coming Out Day would achieve even higher goals in years to come. To this day, HRC has kept its spirit and name alive to educate future generations of Americans who come out, and their families, friends, and co-workers who welcome them.

We believed along with Eichberg and the Human Rights Campaign that coming out was a far more significant first step than simply youthful self-awareness, and, in fact, for most people it is a lifelong journey. We also know that individuals of any age who are open and honest about their sexual orientation have tremendous potential to make lasting change, become politically involved, educate their families and friends, and be valuable role models.

We knew that it was far more than "feeling good"; it also was about doing good. The current outreach, using the now-famous

FIGURE 1.1 Keith Haring design for National Coming Out Day

Source: Human Rights Campaign. Used with permission.

Keith Haring illustration, was not sufficient to reach the diversity of gays and lesbians across the nation and in different stages of their coming-out process.

Too often we realized that the connection between self-awareness and public visibility was strained by personal ignorance, isolation, or self-deception. Younger and even older gay people too often accepted or believed the degrading things others, including their own families, said about them, and simply hid behind their low self-esteem, shame, and fears.

The organizers retained us to communicate awareness about National Coming Out Day and to use our marketing communications know-how to expand its reach and reputation as an educational force among GLBT people.

How could gays and lesbians change society or their community if they could not even be themselves? How could they

FIGURE 1.2 Updated logo for the Human Rights Campaign's National Coming Out project

Source: Human Rights Campaign. Used with permission.

vote for change if they were not willing to change themselves and those who are closest to them? Survey after survey showed that growing acceptance of gays and lesbians is directly tied to knowing someone gay or lesbian.

Our approach was integrated through a complete marketing communications strategy—public and media events, advertising, personal appearances, and community-based networks. National Coming Out Day needed to take its own next steps.

Keep in mind, this all unfolded prior to the possibilities and dynamic spread of the Internet, which was quickly embraced by young gays and lesbians. However, in the pre-Internet world, the tactics were a bit different. Most of the public educational events took place on college campuses and at community centers, where organizers could spread the message to an identifiable group of people. How could we reach even further and leverage the power of the media to help us carry this message?

Fortunately, we soon identified two talented celebrities who were bold and smart enough to join our team and actively take part in the national strategy—Amanda Bearse and Dan Butler. At that time, Amanda already was a successful, gifted, and bright member of the cast of Fox Television's *Married with Children*, and is believed to be the first actor on a prime time show to come out publicly. Soon after, Dan, a writer, actor, director, and legendary

FIGURE 1.3 Cover of *HRC Quarterly* magazine featuring campaign to urge gays and lesbians to vote in the 1996 election

Source: Human Rights Campaign. Used with permission.

"womanizer" made famous for his role as Bulldog Briscoe on NBC's *Frasier,* came out as well.

Bearse and Butler are unique and talented individuals and bridged the secret gap in their lives and were established as openly gay actors—a rarity in Hollywood in 1993, and even today. They no longer lived or worked inside a closet, and found loyal and supportive audiences on television.

Both entertainers played totally believable and popular heterosexual characters, as have many popular gay and lesbian performers over the decades. Hiding one's true sexual orientation so often comes naturally to gays and lesbians, who learn to hide their cues, behavior, and attractions in public and private.

FIGURE 1.4 Ad campaign for National Coming Out Day featuring openly gay actor Dan Butler

Source: Human Rights Campaign. Used with permission.

We knew both actors shared our passion about giving back to the community and serving as role models, and, therefore, we were delighted when they accepted the invitation to be the first-ever national spokespersons for National Coming Out Day. Accepting this pro bono role, each generously took part in ad campaigns, appeared in posters intended for college campuses and workplaces, delivered remarks at HRCF benefits and offered drop-bys, along with other personal appearances and media interviews.

Given their well-known television roles, we crafted just the right message too. In all of our posters and statements, Dan and Amanda both proudly declared, "I'm not a straight person, but I play one on TV." Before that moment, no actor in America had ever made that claim so public and so popular.

The power of celebrity is well known in our society. Their voices have resonance with a large audience, namely their fans. They can serve as important role models, especially for young people.

For young men and women who are grappling with sexual identity, Amanda and Dan were among the first to do so at the top of their careers and at a time when there were far fewer gay and lesbian characters on television (and not one openly gay or lesbian actor).

Over the years, we were blessed by working successfully with several other outstanding role models who emerged to volunteer as spokespersons and activists, including former House Speaker Newt Gingrich's half-sister, Candace Gingrich; Sonny and Cher's daughter, Chastity Bono; Greg Louganis; *Party of Five* actor Mitchell Anderson; Ellen Degeneres's mom, Betty DeGeneres; and later—though not specifically as part of the National Coming Out Project—*Queer as Folk* actor Bobby Gant. We enjoyed our contributing role in writing speeches for most of them and working often to promote their appearances and help leverage their considerable star power for community organizations and their missions.

Each one gave generously to the cause in their own way through public speaking, appearances, college tours, and interviews. Eventually, Candace Gingrich joined the staff of the Human Rights Campaign full time where she continues to be an organizer and evangelist for the GLBT community and for coming out. Over the years, the National Coming Out project wisely matured into a year-round education initiative of the Human Rights Campaign Foundation, too.

American Airlines Finds Its Flight Path

As we embarked on our marketing and media outreach for gay Americans, a second remarkable moment occurred during that first year we started business. One afternoon, we received a telephone call and an invitation to come to Dallas from a friend and former colleague, Tim Doke, then serving as corporate communications director for American Airlines.

Doke's question to us was simple. Could we help advise American Airlines how to navigate and help resolve the mounting tension among AIDS activists and harsh questions from the gay community that challenged American's policies and reputation? At that moment, there was an excellent chance a global backlash or even a boycott might be launched against American Airlines.

We were aware of the reasons why, and had followed the specific events that led to this distressing scenario, because they had been the subject of scathing news stories in the gay and mainstream media. The publicity was unmistakably disturbing and distracting for American Airlines, as it would be for any corporation.

It all started in June 1993 when many GLBT Americans traveled to Washington, D.C., to take part in the March on Washington. Naturally many chose to fly from distant cities, and many flights were crowded with gays and lesbians on American Airlines and other carriers coming to the nation's capital. The same flights were just as full when the gay participants departed on their flights to return home.

One flight that stood out, however, included an enthusiastic and openly gay group of passengers homeward bound to Dallas-Fort Worth on American Airlines. Regrettably, a poorly educated and insensitive member of the flight crew recommended that all of the aircraft's pillows and blankets used by these travelers be consigned to rubbish or be systematically sanitized.

The reason: Misguided fears that the blankets and pillows used by the gay travelers would likely be contaminated with HIV and therefore potentially spread the AIDS virus to the flight crew and other unsuspecting passengers. Word leaked swiftly about this thoughtless gaffe, and was widely reported in many gay news publications. The national gay news magazine, *The Advocate*, published an article entitled "The Ugly American."

As offensive and ignorant as that flight crew warning sounds, matters became even more serious later in the year in a separate but somewhat related incident, when a passenger living with AIDS was removed bodily from an American Airlines flight leaving Chicago one afternoon that fall.

The passenger was visibly frail and in the later stages of an AIDS-related illness. While the flight was boarding, he decided to take his much-needed medication, which at the time was delivered by intravenous injection. Because of the crew's legitimate fears for this individual's safety combined with logistical confusion managing the passenger's intravenous drug therapy, the unfortunate decision was made to insist the passenger step off the aircraft as the crew and gate agents determined if he was well enough to travel.

Tempers grew very short. When he simply refused to move or be moved, the struggle resulted in a much-publicized removal from the airplane by local authorities and eventually a class-action lawsuit. Again, insensitivity and poor internal communications reflected on American's policies and education practices for treating all of their customers with dignity and respect—including passengers living with HIV and AIDS.

For the gay press, both incidents together offered a field day of recriminations and anger. American's path was strewn with militancy on the part of gay and AIDS activists, many stirring up popular opposition to ever flying American Airlines again.

All of these thoughts were on our minds when we arrived at American's corporate headquarters in Dallas. We realized our diagnosis would not be an easy one or solutions readily apparent. We needed to know, of course, whether these incidents were isolated or part of a pattern. Even if both missteps were unforeseeable, had the company's management taken the immediate proper steps afterward to resolve, apologize, and reconcile? We wondered what American Airlines really stood for, and whether we could defend the company effectively in the battle for favorable public opinion.

We also wondered why these scenarios weren't foreseeable or at least included in their internal education and insight. Had the company invested in its employee training to ensure there is no confusion or ignorance about the identity of their customers and their own employees living with HIV and AIDS?

It worried us to imagine that HIV/AIDS was defined or understood by some employees as exclusively a contagion of gay men, leading some to mistakenly confuse sexual orientation purely with HIV status. Clearly, there was much health ignorance not only at this company but very likely within many major corporations, especially ones that promise quality customer service to all. We saw firsthand, and American Airlines immediately acknowledged, that there was a gap in the training and knowledge of flight crews and others who deliver customer care.

In our first face-to-face meeting, we therefore made it clear we were powerless to simply communicate American Airlines' gay welcome, or to shine its reputation once more. The bigger and more immediate priority was internal self-examination, and to understand what substantive steps the company could take to align its policies and practices to ensure future incidents would never occur (or, more realistically, would be extremely unlikely). As communicators, we knew that we had to communicate genuine substance.

From the very beginning, we quickly learned that the leadership was committed to righting these wrongs. It was not lip service but a desire to make their workplace and their airplanes welcoming places for all passengers, including gay and lesbian passengers.

Mistakes happen to us all. No company is immune either. However, we are judged much more by how we respond to them and what remedies we take. That is what often sets true leaders apart. We were determined to capture and characterize American Airlines' true leadership and to endorse a communications strategy that would succeed internally as well as externally.

We believed then, as we do even more today, that how a company puts its own house together is the acid test of how others will perceive and acknowledge its reputation. For gays and lesbians, who often are understandably cynical about corporate intentions and values, this trust is crucial. It is how reputation is earned, measured, and maintained.

Fortunately, we learned that earlier that year, American Airlines had adopted a written statement on employment nondiscrimination that included sexual orientation—one of the first companies and first airlines to do so. Few seemed aware of it, however, and it certainly did not appear to be public knowledge. Yet it represented a solid start.

In addition, we asked whether the company recognized and supported a gay and lesbian employee resource group, whether it sponsored any gay or lesbian nonprofits, how it tackled diversity issues including sexual orientation, whether it offered AIDS sensitivity and awareness training, and also whether it considered offering equal benefits to the same-sex partners of its employees that are routinely available to married spouses. While fewer companies offered equal benefits in the early 1990s, this trend was beginning to show up on the radar screen among human resource specialists.

We reminded our colleagues at American that it did not matter so much whether these questions were yet unanswered, as long as American Airlines was genuinely determined to examine its approach and to foster a gay-welcoming climate within the company. It was important to know whether they were willing to align their practices with fair-minded policies that recognize and include their loyal gay and lesbian workforce.

With the second incident relating to the passenger living with AIDS, the resulting litigation produced a settlement that accelerated American Airlines' commitment to improve and expand its education and sensitivity training on HIV and AIDS. We argued that it made as much sense to include internal sensitivity about sexual orientation and recommended the company empower its own GLBT employees to be a deeper part of the solution.

We felt strongly that nothing but good would come from this corporate soul-searching, and that a smart company would embrace this approach to improving its reputation and marketability. Communicating values can often be as important as communicating a fair price and outstanding customer service. American Airlines, we believed, could make it a win-win.

Fortunately, American Airlines is exactly that kind of a visionary company. From day one, we learned American has a rock solid commitment to good corporate citizenship. We felt and heard a strong desire on its part to rebuild trust and to regain the support of all its customers and employees, including gays and lesbians.

Notably, one of the first assignments we were given was a test of how to rebuild trust and communicate the company's values. A few short months later, in the spring of 1994, New York City was preparing to host hundreds of thousands of gays and lesbians for two special celebrations. The first was the 25th anniversary commemorating the Stonewall bar riots, which are widely acknowledged as the start of the modern gay civil rights era. In addition, New York was planning to host the quadrennial Gay Games, which promote gay sportsmanship and outstanding athletic achievement.

We understandably feared and worked hard to avoid the repeat of any embarrassing incidents involving gay travelers to New York in June when these two events coincided. With many New York–bound planes filled with celebrants, sports fans, and athletes, we recognized that we would have another litmus test to determine whether American really "got it." Fortunately, they really did.

In preparing for those events, our immediate task was to script a company-wide employee training video that then would be narrated by one of American Airlines' top executives. The prescription and words we scripted enabled the company to communicate American Airlines' policies and respectful approach toward all passengers, including those living with conditions such as HIV and full-blown AIDS, and also to teach flight crews and all customer-care employees how to distinguish and respond to their needs more thoughtfully and sensitively.

We took one more giant step forward by also educating all of the employees about the historic events in New York and reminding them that thousands of gay and lesbian visitors would be coming to the city for these occasions. In those historic seven or eight minutes, for the first time ever, an executive at American Airlines literally spoke to and on behalf of all of its gay employees and extended a warm welcome to all lesbian and gay passengers who chose to fly on their planes.

That week thousands of employees in markets across America watched the brief instructional video and received the dramatic educational message; countless gays and lesbians who work at American also told us how touched they were, and how much those first powerful words really mattered to them. For many, it was validation from their employer that they were included, respected, and truly valued. To some, that may seem like a small gesture, but for thousands of airline employees—many hiding their true identities as a lot of gays and lesbians do—it was a bright, hopeful light of things to come.

Starting off with a few words and compiling an unsurpassed track record have made American Airlines' brand and reputation even more secure. Over the next decade, that story has become well known, especially among gay consumers who consistently rank American Airlines as their most popular airline choice. Many of its giant steps are part of this compelling history.

- American Airlines was among the first airlines to adopt written nondiscrimination policies that included sexual orientation in its employee recruitment and retention practices; it later became the first airline to add transgender employees as well.
- American Airlines was the first airline to implement the same partnership benefits for same-sex partners of lesbian and gay employees that it extends to the married spouses of heterosexual employees. It also ensures that the domestic

partners of gay customers have equal membership privileges at airport-based Admirals Clubs, just as married spouses enjoy.

- American pioneered the first dedicated sales and marketing team for gay customer service by adopting its own Rainbow TeAAm, and has served as official airline for more gay and lesbian nonprofits than all of the other U.S. airlines combined.
- By urging the creation of a loyal gay and lesbian employee resource group, Gay, Lesbian, Bisexual and Transgender Employees at American (GLEAM), American Airlines also fostered a vocal employee diversity council that allows GLEAM to partner with other like-minded, diverse employee groups representing people of faith, African-Americans, Hispanics, women, and others.

Regarding HIV and AIDS, American Airlines also flew into the lead by doing its homework; incorporating excellent and detailed curricula into its training materials; sponsoring the mission of national and community leaders battling AIDS, including AmFAR, AIDS Action Council, and the San Francisco AIDS Foundation; and, closer to home, supporting care delivered through community-based AIDS service organizations. American's medical director also served on the board of the National Leadership Coalition on AIDS, an organization dedicated to helping the business community respond to AIDS in the workplace.

What began as a difficult year of turbulence, confusion, and ambiguity about American Airlines' true character was transformed into a decade-long testament to respect, partnership, and crystal-clear communication by the corporation.

Our original strategy had a long-term vision to sustain American's reputation as a way to build business, profitability, and overwhelming support from customers who travel a great deal and have many carriers competing for their travel budget. While service and price matter to everyone, including gay consumers, we saw that corporate reputation had tremendous power to generate enduring and profitable loyalty.

FIGURE 1.5 American Airlines advertisements targeting GLBT consumers

Source: American Airlines. Used with permission.

It is important to note that incorporating GLBT issues into the diversity strategy of the company reaped huge dividends for American Airlines. Over the past 12 years, American can attribute millions in revenue from its targeted outreach to gay and lesbian consumers. Doing the right thing is truly good for business.

American Airlines "invented" frequent flyer concepts as a way to build and sustain their brand for all travelers; more than ten years later, we believe American's gay-respectful reputation is equally vital to sustaining that profitable brand within the gay community.

In those first weeks and months, we learned a great deal about the lasting value of reputation, and the kind of practical lessons that still matter to us every single day. Our goal for the future was to bridge the gaps between companies such as American Airlines and causes such as National Coming Out Day to communicate, educate, and build the reputations of both.

To do so, we needed to explore much more about the marketplace and about the mysteries, hype, and invisibility of gay, lesbian, bisexual, and transgender consumers too. We were determined to learn as much as we could. Only by learning could we then become teachers and expert communicators ourselves.

CHAPTER 2

Evolution of Gay Consumers

No Jews welcomed. No Negroes allowed. No Chinese. No Indians. No Mexicans.

As disturbing as these cruel statements look to our contemporary eyes, they echo eerily from America's history of segregation, exclusion, and discrimination. For decades, signs and messages like those in shops, schools, public transportation, hotels, and restaurants painfully reflected America's intolerant culture, social practices, laws, and apartheid-style economy. Sometimes these signs were written in far coarser and plainer and uglier words.

While undertaking nearly four centuries of nation building and forming social institutions, many Americans created walls, barriers, and prohibitions to stop "others" from fully participating in life's opportunities and practical necessities. Segregating by race, ethnicity, and religion was a conscious act and accepted by many Americans for far too long.

For each of these marginalized populations, the inevitable progress of civil rights and the maturing marketplace have swept away most of the signs, symbols, and laws of exclusion. True inclusion is not yet a reality in all parts of our society; however, we have witnessed a sea change in the last half-century in ending overt forms of discrimination, especially in public life and in our commerce.

For many of the stigmatized populations, most living apart from others, they often created their own economies, with distinct neighborhoods, shops, institutions, clubs, and houses of worship. Separate and apart from the mainstream culture, they often survived and sometimes even thrived on creating market-places and livelihoods entirely their own.

Keen competition combined with growing social awareness and acceptance has changed the face of our economy, and, for the most part, all households today represent valuable consumer opportunities for all businesses. Is there a corporation, a shop owner, a restaurateur, or an Internet entrepreneur today that can truly afford to turn away one customer, let alone an entire group of Americans? Bigotry and exclusion has its cost, and for most businesses, that cost is just too high. Every single customer matters today.

What about subtler and less visible forms of discrimination and separatism? If same-sex couples always remained unwelcome and uninvited, why were there no signs in store windows or hotels and restaurants that declared "no homosexuals," "no queers," or "no faggots"? The explanation is probably a very simple one.

Few establishments even thought it necessary to publicly declare homosexuals unwelcome, because it was always tacitly understood they were uninvited and unwanted everywhere. Outdated laws and long-accepted custom had made it so. Police raids often targeted bars, restaurants, and private clubs, and made harassment, bribes, and humiliation a costly way to do business for so many that tried. Newspapers reporting police raids labeled the arrested individuals as "perverts" or "degenerates." Gays and lesbians complied largely by remaining invisible and "in the closet," and day to day by being able to pass for someone they were not. Even outdated postal laws criminalized the mere act of writing, publishing, and mailing homosexual newsletters, magazines, and mailers.

If homosexuality was famously declared the "love that dare not speak its name," then society simply assumed it was neither necessary nor acceptable to publicize when and where homosexuals were shunned. Most Americans simply assumed it was the unwritten and unspoken code of business as much as society by freely choosing to deny respect, jobs, service, information, goods, entertainment or accommodation to gay people.

THE VISIBILITY AND EMERGENCE OF THE GAY MARKET

Gays and lesbians, of course, always have been part of America's story and a vibrant slice of our nation's economy too. In his remarkable academic history of the gay market segment, scholar Blaine Branchik makes visible the three recognizable stages of the gay consumer identity: (1) the "underground" phase before World War II; (2) the community-building period between the war and the 1970s when gay bars, newspapers, and small enterprises emerged; and, (3) the mainstream phase that we've witnessed in the last quarter century.

As an "underground" entity in early 20th century America, the gay economy existed primarily for gay males (and in more rare circumstances, lesbians) as a way to connect privately, socially, and sexually. This was essential, of course, when community institutions offered no welcome at all or even a remote signal of respect. Whether ostracized or criminalized, gay Americans felt the consequences. Their prewar invisibility meant their economy and connections remained almost entirely separate from the mainstream and beyond the reach of local laws and customs that worked to shut down gay gathering places and to arrest and jail homosexuals on morals charges.

Following World War II, with society going through many changes in urbanization, racial attitudes, and gender roles in the 1950s and 1960s, it is not surprising the contemporary gay movement also began to show its face.

THE RISE OF GAY MEDIA

This period saw the formation of early civil rights groups such as the Mattachine Society and the Daughters of Bilitis, as well as legitimate neighborhood bars and coffee houses owned and managed by gay people; and just as important, the emergence of community media such as newsletters and weekly newspapers and magazines, which ultimately enriched the connection between readers and community advertisers.

Before the growth of local print media, gay men and women had long survived and flourished in most hostile societies through private word of mouth, the recommendation of a personal friend, the code words of a private language that told them where to gather, whom to trust, and what to enjoy.

With the arrival of newsletters, early magazines, simple flyers, and newspapers, however, the code of private trust began to change to public visibility. Archaic postal laws that earlier declared homosexual publications "immoral" and ineligible to be sent through the U.S. mail were challenged and eventually overturned. These breakthroughs made it possible at last for gay people to reach one another and to find social venues, neighborhoods, businesses, and entertainment options that were specially intended for them.

Mainstream advertising was not so fast to find its way into gay media channels—largely resistant because many gay newspapers and magazines survived by advertising gay dating profiles, adult services, gay escorts, and often explicit sexual content. Advertisers felt they simply could not take the risk with their corporate image.

Over the years, however, many gay publishers took steps to rein in their adult advertising and editorial content, and also to shield more adult advertising from the news content in many publications. By the 1970s and 1980s, some emboldened marketers found their way into advertisements intended for gay readers in the pages of *The Advocate*, the nation's oldest and most respected biweekly magazine targeted to the GLBT community. Absolut Vodka, for example, was among the earliest enterprises, as well as films, books, apparel, cigarettes, and a few other selective advertiser categories, that discovered the value and opportunity in speaking to gay consumers in the pages of local and national gay media.

FIGURE 2.1 Current Absolut Vodka ad tailored for GLBT audience

Source: Absolut. Used with permission.

Over the years, of course, the categories of advertisers have grown dramatically. For example, in 2005, the *Gay Press Report* published by Rivendell Media and the respected advertising agency, Prime Access, disclosed that more than 175 Fortune 500 brands were advertised in gay print media resulting in more than $212 million in revenues for gay community publications.

FIRST ATTEMPTS AT MARKET RESEARCH

Intriguingly, two notable moments converged in 1993—the time we first launched our own business. Both have had significant impact on our work and mission, and both have had lasting consequences for the gay consumer market.

The first was an early yet muddled attempt at market research that took place during the 1993 March on Washington. The second milestone, the creation and popularity of the Internet, became a social and economic watershed for all people and has had special relevance for lesbians and gays.

In June 1993, as we described in our first chapter, Washington, D.C., hosted a popular march to celebrate and advance equal civil rights for gays and lesbians with hundreds of thousands of people in attendance from across the United States. With the then–recently elected President Bill Clinton in office, many gay citizens felt perhaps our time had arrived and decided to come to our nation's capital to march and be counted. With a champion in the White House who told them they were "included in the American Dream," many GLBT citizens imagined a much brighter future and our broadest political visibility in history.

Ironically, the March on Washington telegraphed the gay community's biggest dreams yet led to more setbacks when the Clinton Administration was compelled by conservative opponents to compromise on admitting gays to serve openly in the military. With the adoption of the controversial "don't ask, don't tell" rules, the gay community straddled the political minefield that acknowledged our existence and allowed many gays to serve honorably in uniform provided they keep their sexual orientation secret. Obviously, not all Americans feel comfortable with gays and lesbians being open about whom they really are.

If the American military and large numbers of American veterans remained hostile and resistant to gay visibility, many others were not. That same watershed year saw more enterprising companies testing the water and beginning to show up at gay events, fundraising benefits, and community pride celebrations with flyers, T-shirts, tchotchkes, samples, magazines, and promotions.

These early marketers were still largely found among gay-owned-and-welcoming community businesses such as bars, restaurants and caterers, cleaning services, gyms, and spas that knew their loyal gay customers very well and simply wanted to find many more. Swelling their numbers were local bankers, insurance agencies, and other professional service providers.

One curious episode also arose during the 1993 March on Washington with the arrival of Overlooked Opinions, a self-styled market research company. Its research approach and objectives were simple—to sample a cross-section of participants at the march and find out much more about the demographics, consumer preferences, and household habits of all gay consumers. After all, with hundreds of thousands of lesbian and gay activists in one place, how could they miss such a golden opportunity?

Overlooked Opinions was absolutely right about the prevailing ignorance about the gay community. We agreed there were significant gaps in knowledge, understanding, and measurement of gay households. Without accurate data and greater insight about the GLBT population, we knew firsthand it was impossible for corporate decision makers and marketers to take us as seriously as we wished. How can you design a business case without solid metrics about the households you are trying to reach?

We asked ourselves the same kinds of questions that were considered by some pioneering marketers at companies looking to understand this newly emerging market segment: How many gays, lesbians, bisexuals, and transgender people are there? Where do they live? Where do they work? Where do they shop? How many are coupled? How many are raising children?

We wanted to learn how they make basic choices about insurance, doctors and healthcare, cameras, automobiles, computers, apparel, childcare, entertainment, travel, banking, and everything else. Were they just about the same as everyone else? Or are there distinctions and life stages that set gay people apart? Are they touched by advertising that speaks to them directly? How do they know if a company is gay-friendly, simply disinterested, or truly hostile?

We discovered, however, that the techniques used by Overlooked Opinions for its study were as simple and, unfortunately, as misleading as its hopes and expectations. It enlisted volunteers and hourly-paid workers to stream through the gay crowds attending the march and invite each person to spend a few minutes filling out a postcard with private details about their personal income, spending traits, and demographic and geographic profiles. It was intended that the cards would be gathered on the spot or, alternatively, mailed back to the originators for eventual hand tabulation.

There are no details available about the actual number of cards that were completed and returned (or presumably the ` thousands also discarded). The powers that be at Overlooked Opinions, however, seem to have faithfully tabulated the returned information given to them at the march, and released its findings later that same year. Its measures were met with delight, surprise, and even the consternation and confusion of many others.

In breathless prose, it reported that America's gays and lesbians are among the nation's affluent elite. It naively projected the entire sample at the march to be a true and faithful reflection of the nation's gay and lesbian populations as a whole, and, therefore, reported they are much more likely than other Americans to earn extraordinarily high incomes. Overlooked Opinions painted a sharp picture that suggested the consequences of long-standing social and legal discrimination had never held gays and lesbians back from achieving superior economic potential. Worse, it imagined that the gay activists who attended the march somehow reflected all gays and lesbians throughout America.

Of course, that was not the last word by far about Overlooked Opinions' findings or methods. Before the ink could dry, the distorted survey was challenged by scores of activists and academic researchers who asked how a self-selected sample of gay activists could accurately represent all gay households. Many immediately discounted the ballyhoo.

It stands to reason that the individuals participating in the March on Washington seemed largely unburdened by the cost of travel and the expense of accommodations in Washington, D.C., and were certainly more likely to be well-informed, educated, and politically involved and aware than other gays and lesbians or their heterosexual counterparts. There likely was nothing "average" or typical about these participants.

In short, while the findings by Overlooked Opinions may have been accurate, they only reflected a narrow slice or limited cross-section of a more affluent lesbian and gay population. Like other forms of consumer research, there is some value in these findings; but there are obvious limits to what we have learned and how we may wisely use this information. With skewed approaches like this one or magazine readership studies that also target a small proportion of individuals, it is not likely we will find a true picture of the entire gay consumer population or of all gay and lesbian households.

The use of this flawed data as representing the "norm" for the gay and lesbian population was evidenced during Congressional hearings on legislation to protect gays and lesbians from discrimination in the workplace. For close to a decade, civil rights advocates have been working to add sexual orientation to the protections in Title 7, which protects certain classes of Americans regarding workplace hiring, firing, and promotion. Sexual orientation is not one of those classes currently protected.

In the hearings, opponents of the legislation quoted the Overlooked Opinions statistics that stated the average income of gays and lesbians to be much higher than that of the average American. The argument, therefore, was that gays and lesbians needed no protections because their incomes were not impacted negatively as a result of their sexual orientation.

GAYS AND LESBIANS FLOCK ONLINE

Coincidentally, during the summer of 1993 and the years that immediately followed, while Washington swarmed with gay slogans, marchers, and tourists, many gays and lesbians at home began to discover other ways to connect by finding their way curiously and safely to the online world.

With commercial pathways such as America Online that were easy to find, navigate, and use, gay households swiftly discovered how powerful it was to anonymously and safely build connections and relationships with others on the Internet. For young people, in particular, it became a safe and imaginative way to explore their feelings and chat with others who made them feel okay about their identity.

It was not surprising to learn that billboards, e-mail, and chat rooms made it possible for many of the most curious and closeted in the so-called gay community to find others. While hundreds or thousands could afford a trip to the March on Washington, attend gay pride events, or frequent gay bars, the Internet opened affordable, private doorways to millions more. The closet experience was transformed into a virtual experience, with many gays and lesbians communicating with others honestly and openly.

Consider the social climate then—and now. In 1993, and as it remains today, it was perfectly legal in most U.S. states to fire someone simply for being gay, lesbian, bisexual, or transgender whether or not they were well qualified to perform their job. Too often parents and certain religious leaders continue to routinely condemn homosexuality and deny faith, comfort, and support to the gays and lesbians among us.

For gay teens, there remains a terrible and unacceptable epidemic of suicide and patterns of substance abuse as they seek community and protection from the stigma and hostility they find. Also, there were few laws, and no law at the federal level, that protected gays and lesbians against violence directed at them because of their sexual orientation. It is no wonder the Internet swiftly became a refuge, home, community of family and friends, and, of course, sexual release for so many gays and lesbians.

The anonymity of the Internet provided a much-needed safe haven for gays and lesbians who had the simple and human desire to date and form close relationships in a safe way. This ensured that gays and lesbians disproportionately would travel online to meet others, ask questions, make friends, and find services and information that addressed their unique circumstances—all from the privacy and safety of their living room. Where they once had depended largely on local newspapers, word of mouth, local organizations, and businesses, suddenly they had a virtual community and market that knew no geographic boundaries or space or social stigma.

Given the serious limitations and skew found in the sampling of gay consumers by Overlooked Opinions and other narrow studies, we believed there had to be a more credible and authentic approach. Why not establish one that marketers, academics, and the public will trust? With the rise and dynamic growth of the Internet, and the millions of gays and lesbians who adopted it almost overnight, it became clearer to us that a new window had opened to help us study, learn about, and connect with millions of gay households.

The road to credible research is neither simple nor clear. In our next chapter, we'll address the complex dimensions of sexual orientation that have stymied researchers and marketers for years. However, these are questions that must be answered in order for business to develop its strategies, and for our work to craft communications that reach GLBT households effectively.

CHAPTER 3

The Essential Role of Research

Social scientists, demographers, and epidemiologists face daunting challenges when they attempt to count gay Americans. So do the rest of us. And many have tried, beginning with the early efforts of groups like Overlooked Opinions.

Imagine the added challenge in examining their lives, intimate relationships, consumer behaviors, households, and family structures. Over the past decade or so, market researchers and political pollsters have become equally determined to understand the consumer preferences and voting behaviors of gays and lesbians.

Where do we begin to find and identify gays and lesbians? What about bisexuals, transgender people, and individuals who are entirely unsure yet question their sexual orientation? Is "being gay" a preference, an orientation, an aberration, or a phase (as some casually suggest)? Are there fewer or more than one in every ten people? In a 2002 Gallup Poll, a cross-section of Americans were asked directly how many gays and lesbians there are in the population; perhaps somewhat surprisingly, they declared that one in five of us are gay.

For our purposes, we refer frequently to the GLBT population as including all nonheterosexuals who also are sometimes referred to as sexual minorities. We generally rely on definitions characterizing sexual orientation recommended for usage by the National Lesbian and Gay Journalists Association (NLGJA).

35

- Sexual orientation refers to an individual's sexual, romantic, or affectional attraction to the opposite sex, the same sex, or both.
- Homosexuality is defined as the tendency or orientation to be sexually and/or romantically attracted to members of one's own sex.
- A homosexual is a man or woman who tends to find emotional and sexual fulfillment with members of the same sex. The term *homosexual* is most appropriately used in clinical, medical, or sexual contexts. For most purposes, therefore, we use the more popular and widely accepted expression, *gay*.
- A bisexual is an individual who finds emotional and sexual fulfillment with members of either sex.
- When used on its own as a noun, the term *gay* refers solely to male homosexuals.
- The term *lesbian* refers exclusively to female homosexuals and is used as both a noun and an adjective.
- Many research studies define the gay and lesbian population as consisting of gay, lesbian, bisexual, and transgender (GLBT) individuals in order to encompass the continuum of individuals who do not self-identify as heterosexual. The NLGJA also defines *transgender* as "an imprecise term for individuals who cross gender lines. Sometimes synonymous with transsexual and sometimes also including transvestites."

For our purposes, and throughout this book, unless otherwise described, we use the term *gay* as a general descriptive for the GLBT population.

Without question, stigma, family rejection, legal discrimination, countless forms of bigotry, and threats of violence have long made it difficult for sexual minorities to truthfully disclose their identity not only to others but also themselves. For many gay people, the protection and anonymity of staying "in the closet" and not disclosing their true identity is an enduring reality. Confusion about the extent and the nature of sexual orientation has confounded many experts from long before Dr. Alfred Kinsey's time to our own.

These conditions underscore this basic question: How can we best identify, count, and question individuals who so often choose not to be recognized, let alone observed and accurately counted?

Marketers share this conundrum; while they are determined to connect with all their customers, including gays and lesbians, they often must struggle to find them, even in our midst. Fortunately, that puzzle is being solved year after year.

NEW RESEARCH UNLOCKS KNOWLEDGE

Remarkably and despite persistent obstacles, there is a growing body of knowledge and new research data that reflects the increasing visibility of gays and lesbians. This progress is helping to replace myths with reality by offering a more complete snapshot of a highly diverse population of gay, lesbian, bisexual, and transgender consumers. Newer scientific methodologies are evolving that enable us now to query gays and lesbians with a higher degree of safety, certainty, and anonymity, combined with growing confidence in the projectable research outcomes.

Starting in the mid–20th century with Dr. Alfred Kinsey and his pioneering 10-percent benchmark of same-sex behaviors among U.S. males, many researchers have attempted to perform their own counts using a wide range of useful, albeit similarly flawed, tools—from the General Social Survey (GSS) to far more amateurish and less scientific intercepts in the 1980s and 1990s at community events such as Gay Pride festivals, and through gay magazine readership analysis and postcard surveys, such as the one performed in 1993 by Overlooked Opinions.

In recent years, we have benefited from the much-improved 2000 U.S. Census measure of same-sex households, as well as conventional telephone polls, voter exit polls, and online surveys.

Regrettably, we believe early market researchers too often distorted and hyped the GLBT population by overemphasizing the highly visible gay white urban male. This segment of the population arguably is the most open and most "out," and therefore comprised a larger portion of magazine subscription lists and is the likeliest to attend gay community events. This skewed research too often relied on unbalanced samples taken primarily from gay magazine readership surveys. Troubling and overblown generalizations about the entire gay population quickly followed.

Besides misleading marketers, these distortions had other unintended consequences. At times, this mythology that exaggerated wealth and privilege among gays resulted in unwarranted public policy side effects. Some suggested that forms of economic, social, and political discrimination against gays and lesbians were nonexistent at worst or overstated at best. Poor data collection and weak assumptions so often influence poor analysis and policy decision making.

Fortunately, through advanced survey techniques and peer-reviewed examination by leading social scientists—such as Dr. Edward O. Laumann at the University of Chicago, Dr. Lee Badgett at the Institute of Gay and Lesbian Strategic Studies, Dr. Caitlin Ryan at San Francisco State University, Dr. Gary Gates at the Williams Project at the University of California at Los Angeles, Dr. Katherine Sender at the University of Pennsylvania, Dr. Ken Sherrill at Hunter College, Dr. Gregory Herek at the University of California (Davis), Dr. Tracy Tuten Ryan at Virginia Commonwealth University, and others—we are achieving a richer, more complex, and certainly more accurate picture of gays, lesbians, and bisexuals through reexamined and newly emerging social science.

Marketers also benefit significantly from these academic perspectives and foster like-minded investigations about gay and lesbian households by tracking attitudes in the workplace and in commerce to understand the similarities and contrasts with the nongay population.

SEXUAL ORIENTATION FROM MANY DIMENSIONS

When we speak about sexual orientation, and refer to gays, lesbians, bisexuals, and transgender individuals, what do market researchers mean? Do we have common assumptions?

Fifty years after Dr. Kinsey questioned college students and convicts, among others, we now may credit Dr. Edward Laumann and his colleagues for their breakthrough work, *The Social Organization of Sexuality* (University of Chicago, 1994), which characterizes homosexuality along three distinct dimensions: identity (how individuals self-label their sexual orientation), the expression of same-sex desire, and same-sex behavior.

Many studies, especially those conducted by professionals in the field of public health and social science, tend to narrowly define homosexuality in terms of whether an individual specifically engages in same-sex sexual behavior. However, for the purpose of establishing a deeper understanding of the gay and lesbian population, this behavioral approach is inappropriately narrow because it does not take into account the other aspects of sexual orientation.

There are at least two other ways to define a sexual orientation apart from heterosexuality that are not confined to same-sex sexual behavior. One is to be sexually and emotionally attracted to members of the same sex, and the other is to self-identify to oneself and others as lesbian, gay, or bisexual. Defining sexual orientation exclusively in terms of behavior does not take into account the fact that individuals may self-identify as gay or lesbian and not be sexually active. Neither does it acknowledge the truth that some individuals engage in same-gender sexual behavior yet never or rarely self-identify as gay or lesbian. An African-American male, for example, may suggest he is on the "down low" while engaging in same-sex behavior but never characterize himself as gay or homosexual.

In a national sample in the 1990s, Laumann and his colleagues posed important questions about same-sex behaviors, partners, identity, appeal, and attraction. The survey subjects were given face-to-face interviews conducted privately and in confidence; however, the questions about sexual behavior, desire, and identity were submitted in writing through in a self-administered questionnaire only at the very end of the interview. The interviewer never saw the answers because the private questionnaire was placed in an envelope and sealed by the respondent before being handed back.

On same-sex behaviors, this remarkable comprehensive study showed that slightly more than 4 percent of women sampled, and nearly 9 percent of men sampled, reported that they had experienced sexual activity of some kind with same-gender partners.

For smart market researchers, of course, more relevant than investigating sexual behavior is the question of sexual identity and whether people declare they are gay or lesbian. If you wish to speak persuasively to a gay consumer, the single most important question to ask is whether the individual self-identifies as gay and what media, messaging, and market channels are most influential for this individual. What really makes a gay customer tick? Is he or she similar to or different from other kinds of customers?

Another important dimension of sexual orientation is the fact that, unlike genetically visible racial characteristics or ethnic traits, sexual orientation is not an attribute that can be tracked or detected at birth or at an early age. For some individuals, sexual orientation or at least sexual attraction does not appear to be entirely fixed but instead appears to be a mutable characteristic. Sexual maturity and awareness awakens at different times for different individuals. The understanding of bisexuality, for example, reflects these characteristics.

Decades ago, the American Psychological Association (APA) successfully removed homosexuality from its list of clinical and treatable mental disorders, and in more recent years, the APA also labeled attempts at reparative therapy (i.e., therapeutic attempts to change one's sexual orientation) as scientifically unfounded and potentially harmful.

Another challenge with finding and tracking individuals based on their sexual orientation has to do with the fluidity of sexuality itself. Is being gay or lesbian simply being attracted to a member of the same sex? Or does it refer only to people who actually have sex with members of their own gender? Does it include people who only sometimes have sex with members of their own gender?

Dr. Laumann's research underscores that the proportion of individuals who express same-sex attraction or participate in same-sex behaviors—whether male or female—are in greater number than those willing to self-identify as gay, lesbian, or bisexual.

Much valid research shows that self-description (i.e., identifying openly as gay, lesbian, or bisexual) remains a very complex process influenced by innate and environmental aspects. For some, particularly males, the process of identifying as gay, or "coming out," appears to take place at a younger age, while for other men and women, the process may not unfold until midlife, if at all.

These observations ought to be qualified to recognize that our culture is shifting in a number of seismic ways. In the future, with increased visibility of GLBT individuals and households, the perception of children and adults has evolved and will change more with time. There is some anecdotal evidence of this shift underway; for example, some adolescent girls and boys are choosing to attend high school proms with same-sex dates, and at times self-identify as bisexual, if not lesbian or gay.

Socialization, family expectations, and cultural norms, of course, play key roles in the comfort and acceptance that any person feels about his or her sexual orientation. Most recent sampling of gays and lesbians, therefore, tends to be slightly skewed toward younger, emboldened individuals (for example, those between the ages of 18 and 54, with fewer proportionately who are 55 years of age and older). Online samples also suggest a wide range of self-knowledge about bisexuality, with a broad range of behaviors and attractions among men and women who self-identify with this label.

WHAT IS GENDER IDENTITY?

Arguably the least understood and hardest-to-find segment within the GLBT population is that of transgender individuals.

Unlike sexual orientation, gender identity and expression do not specifically focus on same-sex or opposite-sex attraction or behavior. This little-ventured territory is newer and will be valuable for sociological and biological research in the years ahead.

Gender identity is how you see yourself socially, how you see yourself interacting in the world you live in: man, woman, neither, combination of both, or fluidly relating as one and then the other. Looking at gender as an identity considers how you define yourself and the meanings that identity creates in your life.

Gender expression is the gendered traits one expresses. It can be congruent or incongruent with one's identity or the roles society has prescribed for the individual.

A transgender individual is one whose assigned gender at birth may differ from the person's own self-perception as a man, woman, or intersexed person (someone with characteristics of both sexes). Simply put, a transgender person does not identify with the born gender but with the opposite gender. Despite being born with female or male genitals, a transgender individual self-identifies as a person with the opposite sex from their born sex.

For accuracy's sake, researchers must take caution to not confuse gender identity with sexual orientation or oversimplify its characteristics or its manifestations.

Population studies have been slow to identify and count transgender individuals, and to include them accurately in samples. With time, however, this may change and provide us with a more compelling and descriptive portrait of these individuals.

Now that we have begun to define terms and explore the meaning of sexual identity, it is possible to ask how many gay people there are after all.

CHAPTER 4

Counting Gays

Census 2000 may be best recalled by the national media and the GLBT community as the "gay census" for its authoritative and far-reaching effort to enumerate same-sex households. Although single gays and lesbians were left out of the count, demographers say the tally of 1.2 million same-sex unmarried partners is the result of the most extensive polling ever conducted of gays and lesbians in America.

These households were identified as those that contained two adults of the same sex, while also carefully ruling out all other family relationships by blood or marriage and any mere associations through joint tenancy (such as a landlord-tenant or roommate circumstances). When other relationships and household characteristics were logically eliminated through a series of precise questions, these same-sex households were identified as "unmarried partners" of the same sex. Demographers reliably classified these individuals as gay and lesbian couples.

Perhaps not surprisingly, according to Census 2000, more than 99 percent of all U.S. counties had at least one household headed by unmarried partners of the same sex. Gay and lesbian couples totaled close to 600,000 nationwide. Roughly one in three lesbian couples and one in five gay male couples also were found to be raising children under the age of 18 in 2000, contrasted with 39 percent of opposite-sex unmarried partners with children. The comprehensive analysis of this demographic data by demographic researcher Dr. Gary Gates (*The Gay and Lesbian Atlas*, Urban Institute, 2004), provides us with the deepest and most valuable portrait yet of same-sex households.

THE MYTH OF GAY AFFLUENCE

Lasting stereotypes about gay affluence are hard to dispel, especially given the publicity surrounding polls such as the 1993 postcard study by Overlooked Opinions. Fortunately, economist and academic Dr. Lee Badgett has dedicated the past few years to a closer examination of existing income and population data on gays and lesbians.

In her book, *Money, Myths and Change* (University of Chicago, 2001), Badgett explores the true diversity of economic life within the GLBT population and the conclusion that lesbians and gay men appear to earn no more than their heterosexual counterparts. Moreover, it appears in some cases gay men may earn less than comparable samples of heterosexual men.

Census 2000, however, does record that same-sex male partner households may earn slightly more than heterosexual couples. This distinction may be entirely based on gender differences rather than sexual orientation, given that men consistently earn more than women, and the finding that same-sex households are more likely to have both partners employed than their counterpart heterosexual couples.

In 2002, the *Newark Star-Ledger* analyzed Census 2000 data and confirmed much of what we have learned from income studies, particularly concerning same-sex couples and their basic household income patterns.

- Gay men in same-sex couples had an income that was 13.1 percent less than that of married men ($48,960 versus $56,368).

- The average income of lesbians in same-sex couples was 39.2 percent higher than that of married women ($40,025 versus $28,748).
- Gay men in same-sex couples had an income that was 22.3 percent higher than that of lesbians ($48,960 versus $40,025).

We have learned that for smart marketers, the characteristics about earnings and presumed affluence are far less important than consumer patterns, behaviors, and preferences. Market researchers today, therefore, focus far more on buying attitudes, brand loyalty, and key traits such as early adopters of new product trends.

These are all attributes that are valuable to understanding differences between gay and nongay consumers and precisely where marketers focus their attention.

Finding hard-to-reach populations, such as the gay, lesbian, bisexual, and transgender population, has always strained researchers and posed costly obstacles to yielding meaningful and scientifically valid samples. Given overriding issues of privacy and stigma, gays and lesbians have traditionally been among the most difficult if not most costly to track through conventional means, such as face-to-face contacts and telephone and mail surveys.

While some market researchers continue to poll at gay pride events or rely on other venues such as gay bars and publications, as pointed out earlier, these samples are understandably problematic because they tend to include only the most open and fearless members of the GLBT population. Companies recognize that these respondents are a subset population, and statistically unrepresentative of all gay and lesbian households.

Likewise, conducting conventional random methods such as telephone surveys have produced a very small incidence of self-identified lesbians and gays—usually no more than 1 percent to 2 percent of any random population. Written surveys may yield as many gays and lesbians as 3 percent in any randomized sample.

THE PROMISE OF ONLINE RESEARCH

In the past several years, with the explosion of the Internet, online survey techniques have emerged as a promising solution because of their convenience, cost efficiency, and privacy safeguards.

Online surveys allow respondents to maintain complete anonymity, allowing many more gays and lesbians to be comfortable with being asked to share their experiences, concerns, and specific details of their lives, partners, households, and spending patterns. Consistently, the incidence of GLBT people among online survey samples appears to range from 6 percent to 7 percent, which conservatively suggests today that as many as 15 million American adults self-identify as gay, lesbian, bisexual, or transgender.

The application of Internet-based survey research methods within the gay and lesbian population has had a significant impact on the extent and reliability of data available about gay consumers. Dr. Lee Badgett, an academic critic of gay and lesbian consumer polls, however, argues that early online studies of gay men and lesbians may have been skewed because individuals owning computers naturally would have higher incomes. Badgett and other social scientists feared simply that the ability to get online has often meant that respondents to online surveys are "well-heeled." While more true at the emergence of the Internet, does the income gap still divide us online?

The income disparity is changing among Internet users, however, and just as critical, there are proven statistical techniques to reduce obvious selection bias from online polling that are critical to surveying hard-to-reach populations such as gays and lesbians, which we will investigate further in Chapter 6.

The Pew Internet and American Life Project gauges that 72 percent of all American adults currently have access to the Internet at home, at their workplace, or at a public site. More important to underscore, it reports that up to 84 percent of all Americans between the ages of 18 and 49 are now online. Clear differences remain due to racial, ethnic, language, age, and geographic barriers; however, the gender differences and usage among men and women clearly seem to have achieved close to parity.

Additional in-depth research suggests that online surveys are demonstrably more representative of the gay population than the outreach samples frequently used by market researchers studying the gay and lesbian population and that are carried out in venues frequented by gays, especially in bars and clubs.

For example, one such useful study on sexual behavior was published in *AIDS Education and Prevention* in 2002 ("Risk among Men Who Have Sex with Men (MSM) in the United States: A Comparison of an Internet Sample and a Conventional Outreach Sample"). Although the sexual orientation of study participants was defined in terms of sexual behavior, this research has significant implications for evaluating the promise and validity of online surveys of gay men and lesbians.

The authors of this academic study concluded that the findings of their research did not validate the assumption that "Internet respondents are younger and more educated than traditionally recruited adult samples." The results of the study were seen to be in line with other studies suggesting that "educational, economic, and employment differences (i.e., the 'digital divide') identified within the general population with regard to Internet use may not be evident among MSM [i.e., men who have sex with men]." The most likely reason for this phenomenon is "the adoption of the Internet by MSM as a safe place to interact without fear of negative social consequences." In simple terms, gays and lesbians are early adopters of the Web and find its virtual community a safe and anonymous place to connect and meet others.

PUBLIC POLICY AND BUSINESS DEMAND MORE ACCURACY IN DATA

In recent years, as GLBT Americans have become more visible, they also have sought fair and equal protections from lawmakers at local, state, and national levels.

Policymakers and partisans began to ask basic questions too. How many GLBT people are there? What protections available to others do they lack? More and more, gay and lesbian issues have become a larger part of American society. There are openly gay teachers, clergy, business leaders, doctors, public officials, actors, and co-workers who connect with the heterosexual world around them.

At election time, exit polls began to ask voters their sexual orientation to get a truer understanding of gay voter attitudes. The same kinds of issues that influence gay voters were increasingly on the minds of gay and lesbian workers too. In fact, the desire to achieve legitimate protection from discrimination was rising faster in the workplace than it was in the realm of legislation.

Soon, businesses recognized they needed to know much more about this increasingly visible market segment. Just as gay voters expressed their unique hopes and aims, as consumers they also showed distinct characteristics that separate them from other consumers, along with other traits that mirror their heterosexual counterparts.

Even in a business environment, the topic of sexual orientation stirs up a great deal of emotion and preconceived notions. Yet, businesses best operate on facts and data, not hunches or anecdotes. Early research hinted that gays and lesbians were very brand loyal and wished to spend their dollars with companies that reach out specifically to them. We knew that talking facts and not fiction to corporate marketers keeps the message focused and the business goal at hand—to increase the bottom line.

Market research conducted online today is a powerful, improving, and valid tool for understanding and mapping GLBT households and for contrasting them with their counterpart heterosexual households. We believe it will become even more useful and more exacting in the years ahead. In the next chapters, we will describe how we tapped innovative market research to expand this knowledge and to enable us to develop actionable strategies for marketers to communicate with the GLBT community.

As public opinion trends underscore, American attitudes, particularly among younger people, are changing very quickly. Experience tells us that the rapid progress made in corporate America and the marketplace shows growing respect and acceptance for gays and lesbians as customers, managers, entrepreneurs, shareholders, and employees.

This improving climate combined with enhanced knowledge will inform public debate among policymakers and help transform ignorance and invisibility into broader social acceptance for one of the world's remaining stigmatized and often misunderstood populations. It serves everyone's interest to foster and advance all forms of research about GLBT people.

In the pages ahead, we will present a thorough understanding of gay buying power as well as a compelling portrait of gay consumers today based on some of the best up-to-date research available.

PART TWO

The Opportunity

CHAPTER 5

Gay Buying Power

In the past few years, as we've reviewed, much of the U.S. news media along with many marketers have frequently touted the reputed high earnings of gay and lesbian households. Some ballyhoo the gay market as a dream market precisely because of its presumed affluence.

It's much more critical for us to ask whether or not this consumer segment is unique and distinct from other consumer populations in the market and whether marketers may connect with this segment more directly than through conventional marketing channels.

The answer we have learned is a convincing yes. As Chapter 6 will illustrate, gay, lesbian, bisexual, and transgender consumers are unusually brand loyal to companies and brands that reach out to them. They appear to have much in common with other consumers, yet certain traits, behaviors, and preferences stand out that make them especially attractive and compelling to marketers.

But let's step back for a moment. It stands to reason that a certain portion of America's gay population enjoys notable wealth and higher-than-average earnings. However, as earlier chapters have revealed, and through the valuable research of Dr. Lee Badgett, Dr. Gary Gates, and others, there is actually little evidence to suggest that gays and lesbians—on average—earn more than others. In fact, there appears to be more compelling evidence that gay men may earn somewhat less than their heterosexual counterparts while lesbians, in some analyses, may earn slightly more than heterosexual women.

The questions that marketers and journalists raise go beyond earnings and income, however. They also focus on the general concept of buying power in particular, and search for understanding about how much economic clout gays and lesbians wield in today's market. When a company chooses to pursue the gay dollar, it naturally wishes to know what kind of market share it is hoping to achieve.

Understanding buying power also is a fundamental way to acknowledge the many valuable day-to-day contributions that gay Americans make as consumers, workers, families, business owners, shareholders, and economic decision makers. Getting this projection right makes a difference to all of us, including marketers.

BUYING POWER STARTS WITH POPULATION

The first sticking point is how to credibly project the actual number of gays and lesbians in the United States. If we know the true dimensions of the gay population itself, we have a far greater chance to understand more about their characteristics, livelihoods, and consumer behaviors—and ultimately estimated buying power.

As we explored in Chapter 4, Census 2000 provides a uniquely accurate though partial-population glimpse by tracking only same-sex couple households, or at least those identified with unmarried adult partners of the same sex. The Census 2000 data does not identify or enable us to accurately track single gay, lesbian, bisexual, or transgender adults. We will assume, absent contrary evidence, that concentrations of same-sex couples will also correlate reasonably well with populations of single or un-partnered gay men, lesbians, bisexuals, and transgender people.

The Gay and Lesbian Atlas, authored by Dr. Gary Gates and Jason Ost and published by the Urban Institute in 2004, provides a superior analysis of the demographics of those who responded to the U.S. Census, specifically gay and lesbian domestic partners.

As we mentioned in the Chapter 4, *The Gay and Lesbian Atlas* underscores that Census 2000 significantly undercounts same-sex couples, and does not include millions of single gay men and lesbians, or gay couples who do not happen to share a common residence. One possible reason for the undercount is because it is still entirely legal to fire someone just for being gay or lesbian in all but 17 states and the District of Columbia. As a result of this legal discrimination and pervasive social stigma, the actual number of people who responded truthfully to the U.S. Census is likely to be smaller than actually exists. We will always anticipate an undercount as long as honesty about sexual orientation remains something of a persistent taboo under law, culture, and custom in society.

In addition, by focusing only on same-sex male and female couples within the U.S. Census, we also seem to lose sight of the bisexuals among us—adults who evidently have strong, though not exclusive, same-sex attraction, desires, and identity and who sometimes enter into same-sex relationships but not as consistently as gay men and lesbians. For the purposes of our analysis, we intend to include gays and lesbians, as well as bisexuals whose current or most recent partner is an individual of the same sex.

Finally, for the purposes of our general market analysis, we have decided not to include transgender adults for two logical reasons. First, transgender people may be either heterosexual or homosexual in their orientation, and therefore do not necessarily have same-sex relationships or attractions.

Second and more significantly, their true number in the population has been very difficult to gauge given the scarcity of credible data. Until we have better data (namely, enough individuals who are counted and self-identify as transgender), we will assume their numbers are likely to be a fraction of 1 percent of the adult population, and, therefore, not at all likely to impact the overall conclusions. This is a specialized and important topic that truly deserves greater investigation and knowledge.

As we discussed earlier, we recognize that social scientists, demographers, economists, and market researchers seem to estimate the likely dimensions of the gay, lesbian, and bisexual population to be between 4 percent and 10 percent of American adults. In addition, in a nation with nearly 300 million people, the U.S. Census Bureau in 2004 estimated 220 million are adults over the age of 18.

Therefore, the most reliable guesses of the population may be as low as 9 million or as high as 22 million gay, lesbian, and bisexual adults. Again, this estimated range includes only adults over the age of 18. Sociologists quickly point out that the age of "coming out" and self-awareness about sexual orientation today seems to emerge at an even earlier age, possibly as young as 13 or 14. For our analysis, however, and considering the role of adult consumers, we conservatively prefer the age of 18 as the marker.

For more than five years, we have studied numerous online samples of all adults while conducting sophisticated research about gay consumer behaviors and preferences with our respected polling partner, Harris Interactive, best known for the Harris Poll. In more than 50 such online samples conducted by Harris Interactive over those years, we were struck by the consistent fact that the percentage of individuals who freely self-identify online as gay, lesbian, bisexual, or transgender has almost always ranged between 6.5 percent and 7.0 percent of every sample. Because of stigma and fears of self-disclosure among many gays and lesbians, even these percentages ought to be considered conservative; however, we are comfortable using 6.7 percent as a reasonable benchmark for the GLBT adult population today.

With 6.7 percent of adults conservatively self-identified as gay, lesbian, or bisexual (with transgender individuals the most challenging to estimate), that also suggests that the adult population may be as high as 15 million, or roughly at the median point between the lowest estimate of 9 million (4 percent) and the highest estimate of 22 million (10 percent). In addition, by 2009, based on current U.S. population growth (and increased numbers of individuals who "come out" in their sexual orientation as gay, lesbian, or bisexual) the size of the gay population may grow as high as 16.4 million adults.

WHAT IS BUYING POWER ANYWAY?

If the size and the characteristics of America's gay population seem elusive, then the concept of buying power itself also seems often misunderstood or poorly described. Let's try to clear that up.

According to economists, simply put, *buying power* is another term for "disposable personal income," which is defined as the total after-tax income available to an individual to spend on personal consumption, personal interest payments, and savings.

Buying power therefore is simply that—the amount of money we have left over after taxes to spend on goods and services, and to save and to pay interest on our debts (such as our home mortgages and automobiles). Some of us probably think of this simply as our "take home pay." On average nationally, according to economists, roughly 85 percent to 86 percent of an individual's total earnings may be considered disposable personal income or personal buying power.

In the 2004 edition of *The U.S. Gay & Lesbian Market* (Packaged Facts, 2004) report that we coauthored with Bob Brown and Ruth Washton, when examining gay buying power, we chose to apply a smart methodology that is consistent with the approach taken by the Selig Center for Economic Growth at the University of Georgia. The Selig Center is widely known for its expertise in calculating the purchasing power of other minority populations such as Hispanics and African-Americans.

This approach uses national aggregate disposable income data that are compiled by the Bureau of Economic Analysis (BEA) of the U.S. Department of Commerce and provide the most comprehensive picture of overall purchasing power in the United States. Gay and lesbian purchasing power is appropriately calculated by allocating a proportion of aggregate disposable personal income to the gay, lesbian, and bisexual consumer segment.

GAY BUYING POWER TOTALS $610 BILLION FOR 2005 AND IS ESTIMATED TO BE $641 BILLION IN 2006

We estimate America's GLBT buying power on the basis of the following reasonable assumptions:

- According to the latest available data from BEA, aggregate disposable personal income for the United States was projected to total $9.1 trillion in 2005.
- Based upon the allocation of personal income across age groups shown in U.S. Census Bureau data, we also estimate that virtually this entire total (99.77 percent) is attributable to the population 18 years old and over.
- The gay, lesbian, bisexual and transgender population also is assumed to account for 6.7 percent of aggregate disposable personal income in the population 18 years old and over, a proportion consistent with the percentage of gay men, lesbians, bisexuals and transgender people in the population as a whole.
- Thus, the buying power of the GLBT marketplace is an estimated $610 billion in 2005 (.067 ¥ $9.1 trillion).

The fundamental assumption behind this estimate of gay buying power is that the segmented population essentially mirrors, more or less, the adult population as a whole in terms of income generation.

However, the following factors suggest that even these estimates of gay purchasing power can be viewed as conservative, especially when applied to gay household purchasing power.

As Census 2000 confirms, same-sex adult couples are more likely to live in urban areas than rural areas and small towns, while gay couples living in major metropolitan areas are more likely to be white than the population as a whole in these areas. Both of these demographic characteristics generally are associated with higher average incomes.

The Census 2000 data also confirms that gay couples are less likely than married heterosexual couples to have children, and they are more likely to have both partners in the workforce. (Census 2000 shows that 57 percent of same-sex couples have both partners working, while this is true of only 48 percent of heterosexual married couples.) These factors result in higher per capita household income, especially in the case of gay male couples.

Census data also characterizes the median household income of same-sex couples as somewhat higher than that of married couples ($60,000 versus $57,900). However, a 2005 Harris Interactive/Witeck-Combs Communications survey suggests that only one in five, or 22 percent, of GLBT households had a child under the age of 18. Because same-sex couples are less likely to be raising children (and therefore, less likely to be spending their earnings on education, health care, goods, and services for offspring), the per capita income of households of same-sex couples is significantly higher (21.9 percent) than that of married couples ($32,656 versus $26,784).

Figure 5.1 contains buying power projections and population estimates between 2005 and 2009, and is modified and excerpted from our projections contained in *The U.S. Gay and Lesbian Market 2004*, published originally by Packaged Facts in 2004.

FIGURE 5.1 Projected Growth in Total Gay Buying Power, 2005–2009

Year	Population (thousands)	Per Capita Buying Power	Aggregate Buying Power (millions)
2009	16,414	$45,366	$744,639
2008	16,119	43,954	708,500
2007	15,831	42,580	674,091
2006	15,549	41,246	641,333
2005	15,264	39,973	610,149

Source: *The U.S. Gay and Lesbian Market 2004* (Packaged Facts and Witeck-Combs Communications)

CAVEATS ABOUT BUYING POWER

Understanding buying power is indisputably useful for economists, business executives, public policy analysts, and those of us who wish to calculate market potential and emerging market opportunities. With $641 billion in estimated buying power for the GLBT community in 2006—growing to nearly $745 billion by 2009—it is no surprise that many Fortune 500 companies are investing more each year to tap this profitable potential and to understand gay consumers.

In terms of niche marketing, comparisons are invariably made among different population groups to calibrate where each one stands against another. Is African-American buying power the most dynamic? Do Asian-American households have more commercial clout per capita than Hispanic households? How do gays and lesbians stack up against the buying power of other population groups?

Before even considering these questions, a caution light must pop up and we must slow down. Certainly there are reliable estimates of buying power for each ethnic or minority population in the nation, according to analyses performed by the University of Georgia's Selig Center. For instance, with a population of 38 million people, in 2005 African-Americans were estimated to have a combined $760 billion buying power. For 42 million Hispanics, their 2005 buying power totals $735 billion.

However, when we estimate the buying power calculation for gay Americans, we must remember these are based only on adults over the age of 18, while ethnic and racial buying power calculations include all members of all ages within each target household beginning with birth. It stands to reason we can accurately identify a person's ethnicity or racial composition at birth, while sexual orientation is a naturally occurring characteristic that only becomes apparent in the later teens or adult life.

It should also be obvious that gays, lesbians, bisexuals, and transgender people come from all walks of life, all ethnicities, and all races. In short, the projected buying power for gay adults includes individuals who will be part of buying power projections for other groups as well, including African-Americans, Hispanics and Asian-Americans. It is therefore difficult, if not impossible altogether, to accurately compare gay buying power with that of other populations without mischaracterizing and possibly distorting the relative strengths of each.

BUYING POWER AS A VALUABLE TOOL

Buying power matters.

Knowing how to identify, measure, and apply aggregate buying power can be a valuable tool that reveals the full measure of economic contributions made by all Americans. Gay, lesbian, bisexual, and transgender people have long participated in the U.S. economy as taxpayers, workers, investors, philanthropists, parents, patients, and consumers. Their earnings, investments, savings, and contributions present a strong barometer of economic vitality. With $641 billion in buying power as the current benchmark, gay Americans will continue to be important players in the future of America's commercial potential and economic growth.

In our next chapter, we then will try to describe those traits, behaviors, and market preferences of gay consumers that show how they sometimes mirror—and how they contrast with and stand apart from—their heterosexual counterparts.

CHAPTER 6

Company Reputation and Brand Loyalty

In Chapter 1, we spoke about why reputation seems to matter so much. We also described some of the ways in which American Airlines chose to navigate its path and, despite many obstacles facing the airline industry today, has learned how to build corporate reputation along with market share.

Beyond these market lessons, we always have wanted to test these fundamental assumptions and ask more basic questions. Who is a typical gay consumer? Is the average gay consumer really more brand loyal than others? What does a company's reputation mean to gay consumers, and how can marketers recognize and tap into this loyalty?

For that matter, can we really identify a typical gay man or an average lesbian? What about bisexuals and transgender people? These are challenging questions to answer, and it is risky to draw hasty or unsupported conclusions.

As we understand from social science, sexual orientation is an innate characteristic found in all slices of America's diverse population. The true incidence of homosexuality appears to be found in all ethnic and racial groups in comparative numbers. It also crosses all geographic and socioeconomic barriers. In other words, gays, lesbians, bisexuals, and transgender people come from all walks of life and every part of society.

In many ways, it seems to us, their consumer behaviors also may mirror their other demographics, such as their ethnicity, gender, or age. It stands to reason that any household is made up of multiple markers or perspectives. Knowing that, we believe research is best applied to learn what factors—more than others—account for consumer choice and brand affinity.

Given these demographic assumptions, marketers must work harder to understand the dynamics of corporate reputation and brand loyalty if they are to reap their growing share of the valuable gay consumer market.

FIRST, UNDERSTANDING THE RESEARCH

To better investigate the concept of brand loyalty and compare gay consumers and their households with all Americans, we established an exclusive research partnership beginning in 2000 with Harris Interactive, the well-regarded polling and market research firm best known for the prestigious Harris Poll. Lou Harris founded his polling company in 1956 and over the past half-century it has blossomed and expanded as one of the leading global research and information companies of its kind. Given its successful innovation through technology advances, the company was renamed Harris Interactive in 1999.

The investigators, statisticians, and social scientists at Harris Interactive work closely with major institutions and important media, such as *USA TODAY* and the *Wall Street Journal*, while performing a wide range of public policy and market studies on health, business, politics, and global change for their corporate and nonprofit clients.

In the 1990s, as we spoke to corporate executives about the GLBT market, they would ask how many GLBT people lived in a specific part of the country, or how GLBT consumers felt about their products or services. Almost all of the market research at this point was derived from readership surveys of gay magazine subscribers, a very self-selected sample of mostly white, urban males.

These same executives would then say, "Until you can provide me better data, I can't justify entering this market." We also sensed corporate America's discomfort and wariness with discussing this issue, which generated even more caution.

In 2000, we set out to fill this yawning gap and identify a market research firm with a stellar reputation that could help us move the discussion about the gay and lesbian market away from the hunches and anecdotes to decisions based on facts. If we could take the emotion out of the discussion and rely on solid facts, myths and stereotypes would begin to dissipate and sound business decisions could be made.

After speaking with a number of leading researchers, we formed a relationship with Harris Interactive, Inc. (*www.harrisinteractive .com*) to delve into the minds and market behaviors of gays and lesbians. We felt this cutting-edge partnership could help educate and empower all of us to shed long-awaited light on the true characteristics and contributions of GLBT Americans in all parts of our economy and society.

Through our unique partnership over the past six years, we have created the single largest and most diverse subpanel of self-identified gay, lesbian, bisexual, and transgender voluntary respondents. Currently, we are approaching 50,000 GLBT adults who have agreed freely to be invited to respond to research inquiries online, and within a larger public sample, to be contrasted and compared with their nongay counterparts. Within the next few years, we hope to reach perhaps as many as 75,000 to 100,000 self-identified GLBT adults to expand our pool of prospects and to enable us to segment samples with increasing skill.

Where did these thousands of gay people come from? How were they found? Like the GLBT population itself, they come from everywhere and reflect the complex and intriguing composition of the entire community. Nearly ten years ago, Harris Interactive created and continues to maintain what we believe may be the largest online panel available anywhere.

Harris Interactive currently maintains a multi-million-member panel tapped from nearly 200 diverse Web sites of general and special subject interest. (Some also are recruited for the online panel by telephone.) It's important to underscore, however, that none of these Web sites today are specifically or exclusively targeted to gays and lesbians and they do not single out sexual orientation as a specific characteristic of Web users when they are first recruited.

We presume, based on our understanding, that gay people truly are found everywhere. It is logical and prudent to recruit diverse gay respondents from a wide array of information and specialty sites, and not isolate our panel to those individuals who merely self-select to enter and visit gay and lesbian Web sites.

Naturally, some of these panelists may indeed visit GLBT Web sites, such as Gay.com, PlanetOut.com, or other popular destinations. However, that was never the criterion or the threshold to determine their inclusion in the panel. We wished to find lesbians and gays anywhere online, not just in places exclusively gay, in order to get a truer sense of the population.

Once an individual volunteers two times to join the larger Harris Interactive online panel, that person can then be invited to choose whether or not to participate in future surveys conducted online, by telephone, or via other methods. If they choose to opt out of the panel at any time, they may voluntarily do so.

Only after joining the national online panel will these individuals be asked more details about themselves, as well as more sensitive or personal questions regarding their earnings or their sexual orientation. If they self-identify as gay, lesbian, bisexual, or transgender when they are queried, then they are made part of the growing GLBT specialty panel.

REDUCING FLAWS FROM ONLINE SURVEYS

How can we find authentic samples of gays and lesbians online that, along with other adults, truly represent the broad diversity and complexity of the population?

Research showed that the incidence of self-identification among GLBT people was much higher online than in telephone surveys. Regularly, we found that roughly 6.5 percent or so of any random online adult sample self-identifies at gay, lesbian, bisexual, or transgender versus only 2 percent in more conventional telephone surveys. Online survey methods clearly were going to provide the greatest amount of accurate, self-disclosed information about the GLBT segment.

Harris Interactive seemed to be well ahead of most other researchers in conducting some of its research online. Its work evolved from the years of research it conducted via telephone, especially the well-known Harris Poll. Each month, Harris Interactive also conducts online surveys of a national cross-section of 2,000 and more adults, aged 18 and older. To generalize online survey results to the overall American population, key demographic variables (e.g., sex, age, education, race, and ethnicity) are applied that are derived from telephone surveys, as well as a variable representing the propensity of an individual respondent to be online—a composite of several behavioral factors. This last weighting is key because not all Americans yet have access to the Internet and not all people may be found online (even if they have Web access). The completed online interviews consistently also are weighted scientifically to reflect baseline figures obtained from the latest U.S. Census.

How do they achieve this? Harris Interactive pioneered an intriguing parallel methodology that enables its researchers to conduct identical polls by telephone and online, and then to determine what behaviors and attitudes are different (and which are the same) between the telephone and online respondents. It stands to reason these two populations may differ in other behavioral and attitude characteristics (in addition to education or social status).

Through this parallel approach with two samples, researchers have been able to weight the responses from online survey participants so that they better mirror some of their telephone counterparts. In day-to-day practice, though understandably not perfect, this innovation has significantly helped reduce some of the inherent and known biases in online research and provides marketers significantly higher confidence in their survey

FIGURE 6.1 Backgrounder describing Witeck-Combs Communications/Harris Interactive research partnership

Source: Witeck-Combs Communications and Harris Interactive. Used with permission.

findings. Simply put, we can say with a higher degree of certainty that an online survey performs reasonably well in measuring traits, behaviors and attitudes of populations—especially the harder-to-reach populations such as GLBT people.

For example, individuals who have access to the Web, yet who are not usually or consistently found online, may spend more

FIGURE 6.2 Witeck-Combs Communications/Harris Interactive ad

Source: Witeck-Combs Communications and Harris Interactive. Used with permission.

of their time in outdoor activities or reading books, or perhaps are a bit more introverted. Some may possibly harbor personal anxieties toward using technology. All of these behaviors and feelings, for instance, may differ between individuals who shun the Internet and individuals who are more frequently online. By studying the propensity of an individual to be online, statisticians can develop workable weighting schemes that take these attitudes and behavioral factors into proper account, much as demographers must do with better known traits such as age, education, geography, race, gender, and so on.

As we pointed out in earlier chapters, the very modest proportion of individuals who self-report they are transgender remains quite small comparatively and it is difficult, if not impossible, to safely generalize findings about this subset of the GLBT population (though we plan to keep trying). In addition, transgender people may be either homosexual or heterosexual in their sexual orientation and behaviors; therefore, they may not always be the most appropriate subjects for knowledge about gay perspectives and same-sex attraction. For this reason, we collect data on transgender individuals but cannot yet say anything statistically accurate about them until greater numbers self-identify or we capture more data and knowledge.

Bisexuals also pose challenges when included in samples of GLBT populations because individuals vary so much in describing their attraction, behavior, and sexual identities. For instance, people who are primarily attracted to the opposite gender honestly may profess to be bisexual, but also disclose they never have had sexual intimacy with a person of the same sex, have never had a same-sex partner, and do not attend gay events, do not read gay magazines, nor do they report that they visit gay Web sites.

We can make a guess that many such bisexuals may feel connected more closely with the predominant heterosexual culture, and, therefore, associate more rarely—whether sexually or socially—with gays and lesbians. Their overriding point of view may be a heterosexual variant, and they may not have the same priorities as a consumer who participates in gay social gatherings and same-sex relationships. In our work with clients, to include bisexual respondents with some success, we tend to qualify the bisexual individuals if their most recent past or current partner is the same sex.

Our online research investigations, therefore, are managed with great care, as well as the sampling conducted by Harris Interactive to include and to contrast both GLBT and non-GLBT projectable samples. Unlike other such panels, we have a higher degree of confidence that participants who self-identify as GLBT come from a diverse and broad range of original sources—and largely avoid self-selecting those recruited mostly or exclusively from gay sites and venues. We believe with reason this thoughtful investigation offers a truer glimpse of the varied and complex individuals who actually make up the GLBT community in America. Moreover, Harris Interactive adheres to the disclosure guidelines recommended by the National Council on Public Polls *(www.ncpp.org)*, which advocates and insists upon a high degree of transparency in terms of their data collection, reliability, and accountability. To fathom the GLBT community truthfully, we would expect no less.

For all these reasons and basic assumptions, we approach market research with considerable care and reasonable caveats. This has helped us to intelligently explore critical concepts and behaviors such as the popular notion of brand loyalty. What makes a gay consumer develop unique brand preferences and loyalty that may be somewhat different from other consumers?

GAY-FRIENDLY BRANDS

The term *gay-friendly* and the expression *gay-welcoming* frequently are touted when discussing marketing products to gay and lesbian consumers. Is this akin to the expressions *environmentally friendly* and *child-friendly* that companies sometimes use to characterize qualities intended to appeal to a certain kind of shopper, such as an individual who is deeply protective of the environment and shops for "green" products or the mother who wants to ensure the products she brings home are not risky for her toddlers? Perhaps, but they also tend to have somewhat deeper meaning among gays and lesbians.

In the past decade, we have learned much about the dimensions of gay friendliness, and how it translates into brand preferences and affinity for GLBT consumers. Based on evidence, we presume that many gay consumers, on average, tend to be more skeptical and more questioning than other consumers. Through their own life experiences, the experiences of gay friends, family members, and colleagues, and their observations from the media and the community, they have witnessed frequent market behaviors that can stigmatize, ignore, or marginalize gay people.

For years, gay consumers have been bombarded with many forms of advertising, speeches, sales letters, appeals, and salesperson behaviors that, at best, never even acknowledge them or at worst, stereotype, demean, or insult them. It is no wonder that until recently, gays and lesbians have not felt included or valued when approached as customers (or employees).

To project authentic gay friendliness, and, logically, to connect with these skeptical consumers, companies have developed specific ways to project their corporate reputation and fair-minded practices to underscore that gays and lesbians are expressly identified and included.

These basic measures include nondiscrimination policies in hiring and promotions; reaching out to gay nonprofits and causes; promoting gay visibility, pride, and acceptance in the company's culture; and, logically, offering equal job benefits to same-sex partners that have traditionally been available to married couples. In addition, many more companies are developing inclusive and respectful advertising strategies that reflect and respect their gay consumers.

To help truly understand what gay consumers look for and expect from gay-friendly companies, over the past few years we have explored awareness by gay consumers of brands that have reached out to them. We wished to find out what attributes make the most difference to the consumer, and the motivation that persuades them to choose one product brand over another. In several polls conducted over the past few years, we have asked relevant questions to GLBT and heterosexual respondents to attempt to get to the heart of it.

For example, in June 2004, to better understand buying behaviors, we asked over 2,000 adults, of whom roughly 6 percent self-identified as gay, lesbian, bisexual, or transgender, this question:

Many companies promote diversity in their hiring and workplace practices. These practices include equal treatment of employees and customers from diverse backgrounds, including race, ethnicity, gender, physical ability, sexual orientation, and religion.

How strongly do you agree or disagree with the following statement? I choose to do business with companies that I know have a commitment to diversity and equal treatment of employees.

	GLBT (%)	Heterosexual (%)
Strongly disagree	1	5
Somewhat disagree	–	5
Neither agree nor disagree	20	32
Somewhat agree	23	25
Strongly agree	55	34

Nearly eight out of ten gays and lesbians agree (compared to six out of ten heterosexuals), with more than half of the GLBT panel strongly in agreement.

In December of the same year, we decided to delve into more specifics by asking the following three questions to determine more precisely what gay consumers find important in choosing a brand:

How likely are you to consider brands that support nonprofits and/or causes that are important to you as a gay, lesbian, bisexual, or transgender person?

Extremey likely	28%
Very likely	22
Likely	14
Somewhat likely	29
Not at all likely	7

How likely are you to consider a brand that is known to provide equal workplace benefits for all of its employees, including gay and lesbian employees?

Extremely likely	**40%**
Very likely	**29**
Likely	**18**
Somewhat likely	**12**
Not at all likely	**2**

How likely are you to consider purchasing everyday household products and services from companies that market directly to gays and lesbians over competing brands that do not?

Extremely likely	**14%**
Very likely	**22**
Likely	**27**
Somewhat likely	**26**
Not at all likely	**11**

As you can see from all three questions, gays and lesbians tend to look even closer at a company's internal practices—how it treats its own employees—as an objective barometer of fairness and welcome.

Of all three considerations, equal workplace practices rank somewhat higher than cause-related philanthropy and marketing directly targeted to gays and lesbians. A company's workplace practices, of course, directly reflect the company's commitment to fairness, and may indicate the truest portrait of a company's sincerity toward gays and lesbians. Is the company really doing the right thing? Or is it merely trying to curry favor and snag more profits from gay customers?

In January 2006, we saw the trend continue to climb when 79 percent of GLBT Americans also said they were likely to consider a brand that is known to provide equal workplace benefits for all of its employees, including gay and lesbian employees.

Common sense likely tells us too that gays and lesbians may not be all that different from their heterosexual counterparts in terms of many market behaviors. For example, gay households remain sensitive to the basic considerations of quality, price, and convenience when shopping. They simply include one more vital factor in their shopping behaviors, and it comes down to the company's intrinsic reputation regarding gays and lesbians.

In addition to approaching this question in a general way, we also have asked respondents to identify the top reasons for their buying preferences among specific product categories, such as banking, airlines, rental cars, discount retailers, audio electronics, automobiles, hotels, and personal computers and software.

Not surprisingly, all adults surveyed—gay and nongay consumers alike—said that regardless of the product category, "convenience" and "friendly and welcoming customer service" were the top two criteria used to discriminate among companies, assuming price, quality, and function are alike.

However, no matter what category of product or service, GLBT individuals consider "equal treatment" of gay employees in the workplace as the third or fourth most compelling reason (depending on the product) to favor one company over another when making their own purchase decisions.

Given the importance of judging corporate character and reputation, in December 2004 we also asked how gay consumers learned about a company's approach. In other words, how do they become discerning about corporate reputation? We asked the following to determine the value of "word of mouth" communication as well as the significance of gay media, both online and in print:

If you wish to be aware about a company's reputation for gay friendliness, where do you look?

Word of mouth	**46%**
Gay Web sites	**30**
Gay magazines/newspapers	**29**

Close friends	26
Gay and lesbian nonprofit organizations	19
Mainstream news sources	11
Advertisements by the company	7
Other general interest Web sites	7
Personal customer experience	5
Gay and lesbian chambers of commerce	5
Family members	5
Other	5

Knowing the understandable sensitivity of corporate reputation to GLBT households, in recent years, the Human Rights Campaign, the nation's largest GLBT civil rights group, has prepared detailed and objective reports about America's largest corporations. These reports are now found within the Web-accessible HRC Corporate Equality Index that clearly shows how each of these companies stacks up in its fair-minded treatment and support for GLBT employees and customers across the board. Companies that match all of the basic fairness criteria, consequently, earn perfect marks. Last year, a remarkable 101 companies earned this very important marketplace standing.

During the December 2005 holiday shopping season, to take this idea logically a step further, the Human Rights Campaign expanded its community education efforts by publishing and distributing thousands of copies of a new *Buyers' Guide* that shows at a glance how marketers measure up in terms of their reputation and performance measures.

Immediately following publication of the guide, we then surveyed more than 400 GLBT adults to determine how helpful this tool was to them, and just how receptive they are to having access to such an objective consumer index. Seven out of ten responded enthusiastically and said that they would strongly wish to use this information to advise them on their day-to-day market choices.

Gays and lesbians have demonstrably grown in awareness and allegiance to those companies that show them full respect

FIGURE 6.3 Human Rights Campaign's Corporate Equality Index

Appendix A | 2005 CORPORATE EQUALITY INDEX SCORES, SORTED ALPHABETICALLY BY COMPANY NAME

Employer Name	City	State	Fortune Rank	2005 Score	2004 Score	"Sexual Orientation" in EEO	"Gender Identity or Expression" in EEO	Domestic Partner Benefits	GLBT Employee Resource Group or Diversity Council	Diversity Training	Marketing, Sponsorship or Philanthropy	No Anti-GLBT Activities
3M Company	St. Paul	MN	105	71	71	✓			✓	✓	✓	✓
A.G. Edwards Inc.	St. Louis	MO		43	43			✓		✓		✓
Abbott Laboratories	Abbott Park	IL	100	71	71	✓		✓		✓	✓	✓
Abercrombie & Fitch Co.	New Albany	OH		71	71	✓		✓		✓	✓	✓
ABN AMRO Holding N.V.	Chicago	IL		86	86	✓		✓	✓	✓	✓	✓
Accenture Ltd.	New York	NY		86	86	✓		✓	✓	✓	✓	✓
Adobe Systems Inc.	San Jose	CA		86	86	✓		✓	✓	✓	✓	✓
Advanced Digital Information Corp.	Redmond	WA		29	29	✓						✓
Advanced Micro Devices	Sunnyvale	CA	387	71	71	✓		✓		✓	✓	✓
Aegon USA	New York	NY		43				✓		✓		✓
Aetna Inc.	Hartford	CT	108	100	100	✓	✓	✓	✓	✓	✓	✓
Affiliated Computer Services	Dallas	TX	460	86	86	✓		✓	✓	✓	✓	✓
Agilent Technologies Inc.	Palo Alto	CA	290	100	100	✓	✓	✓	✓	✓	✓	✓
AIG (American International Group)	New York	NY	9	43	29	✓		✓				✓
Air Products & Chemicals Inc.	Allentown	PA	281	86	71	✓	✓		✓	✓	✓	✓
Albertson's Inc.	Boise	ID	35	71	71	✓				✓	✓	✓
Allegheny Energy	Hagerstown	MD		57	57			✓		✓	✓	✓ /
Allianz Life Insurance Co. of North America	Minneapolis	MN		71		✓		✓		✓		✓
The Allstate Corp.	Northbrook	IL	51	86	86	✓		✓	✓	✓	✓	✓
ALLTEL Corp	Little Rock	AR	265	29	0	✓						✓
Alston & Bird LLP	Atlanta	GA		100		✓	✓	✓	✓	✓		✓
Altria Group Inc. (Philip Morris Companies Inc.)	New York	NY	17	71	71	✓		✓		✓	✓	✓
Amazon.com Inc.	Seattle	WA	303	71	71	✓		✓	✓	✓		✓
American Airlines	Ft. Worth	TX	119	100	100	✓	✓	✓	✓	✓	✓	✓
American Express Co.	New York	NY	62	100	100	✓	✓	✓	✓	✓	✓	✓
American President Lines Ltd.	Oakland	CA		43	43	✓		✓				✓
Amgen Inc.	Thousand Oaks	CA	212	86	71	✓		✓	✓	✓	✓	✓
Anheuser-Busch Companies Inc.	St. Louis	MO	139	86	79	✓		✓	✓	✓	✓	✓
Apple Computer Inc.	Cupertino	CA	263	100	100	✓	✓	✓	✓	✓	✓	✓
Applebee's International Inc.	Overland Park	KS		86	86	✓		✓	✓	✓	✓	✓
Applied Materials Inc.	Santa Clara	CA	270	71	71	✓		✓		✓	✓	✓

www.hrc.org/worklife

CORPORATE EQUALITY INDEX 2005

18

Source: Human Rights Campaign. Used with permission.

and welcome. Given these deepening ties, today we are witnessing the emergence of more and more companies that have chosen to align their corporate philosophy and commitment to diversity with their profitable, niche marketing strategies.

FIGURE 6.4 Human Rights Campaign's *Buyer's Guide*

Source: Human Rights Campaign. Used with permission.

FIGURE 6.4 Human Rights Campaign's *Buyer's Guide* (continued)

INSURANCE & HEALTH CARE

Aetna	100	John Hancock Financial	
Choicepoint	100	Services	93
Chubb	100	Allstate	86
Kaiser Permanente	100	Cigna	86
Lincoln National	100	Guidant	86
MetLife	100	Hartford Financial Services	86
Nationwide	100	Harvard Pilgrim Health Care	86
Allied Insurance		Mutual of Omaha	86
Scottsdale Insurance		Principal Financial Group	86
Titan Insurance		Quest Diagnostics	86
Victoria Insurance		SAFECO	86
○ **Prudential Financial**	100	St. Paul Travelers	86
Prudential Long Term Care		Vision Service Plan	86
Insurance		WellPoint	86
Wells Fargo	100	Associated Insurance	
Wells Fargo Insurance			

UnumProvident	79	PacifiCare Health Systems	64
Allianz Life Insurance	71	Caremark RX	57
State Farm	71	Health Net	57
University Hospitals		Humana	57
of Cleveland	71	ING Insurance	57
Chamberlin Edmonds		Massachusetts Mutual Life	
& Associates	64	Insurance	57
New York Life Insurance	64	Progressive	57

AEGON USA	43
Transamerica	
American International Group	43

72% of GLBT people
prefer brands that support
GLBT causes. Source: Witeck-Combs Communications/Harris Interactive 25

Source: Human Rights Campaign. Used with permission.

GAY-FRIENDLY WORKPLACES

Another determinant of a company's reputation as a gay-friendly company is how well it attracts and retains GLBT employees. In today's competitive job market, companies that have the best and brightest employees are the ones most likely to lead in their industry and in the marketplace.

The high-technology industry was one of the first to recognize this in the mid-1990s, when it offered benefits to its GLBT employees and their partners equal to those already available to married couples. Companies like IBM and Hewlett-Packard (HP) understood that brain power was what distinguished one company from the other. These corporations could not afford to have the brightest graduate from the Massachusetts Institute of Technology turn down a job offer because the workplace was not considered GLBT-friendly or receptive.

Soon, more and more human resources forums included discussions on providing parity for GLBT employees in the workplace. There were companies that led the pack and whose management had lessons to teach. Like IBM and HP, we have observed that other giants like Kodak, American Express, American Airlines, Motorola, and Citigroup are frequently cited as companies that set a higher standard for others to follow. Each had also created GLBT employee resource groups, comprised of openly GLBT employees at each company who provided a voice to management on the concerns and issues most important to GLBT workers and how GLBT-friendly they found their workplace.

Employee resource groups (ERG) have been one of the most effective channels of communication for corporate America to ensure that policies meet the needs of the diverse workforce. ERGs also often represent groups of employees from a wide variety of backgrounds, including women, people with disabilities, African-American, Hispanic, Asian Pacific, and people of faith.

In the late 1990s, three GLBT workplace organizations existed to help provide leadership, guidance, and resources for this emerging workplace need and to combine the voices of many employee resource groups. The alliance was named The Pride Collaborative and included Building Bridges, formed in 1990 to offer lesbian and gay sensitivity training to United Way–funded agencies in the San Francisco Bay Area; AGOG (A Group of Groups), formed in 1994 by employees from a dozen San Francisco Bay Area companies to provide joint networking opportunities for members of their respective GLBT employee associations, also known as ERGs; and Progress, formed in 1995 to provide leadership development resources, including national leadership summits for ERG leaders.

In 1999, The Pride Collaborative merged with COLLEAGUES, a national organization that sponsored the annual Out & Equal conference aimed at human resource professionals and GLBT employees, to form Out & Equal Workplace Advocates. Today, Out & Equal Workplace Advocates champions safe and equitable workplaces for lesbian, gay, bisexual and transgender (LGBT) people. The organization advocates building and strengthening successful organizations that value all employees, customers and communities.

For the fifth year, Out & Equal Workplace Survey has partnered with Harris Interactive and Witeck-Combs Communications to investigate and contrast the attitudes of heterosexual and GLBT Americans related to GLBT issues in the workplace. The Out & Equal Workplace Survey is the longest-running annual survey of its kind.

In May 2006, the latest online survey of over 2,000 U.S. adults found that the benefits a company offers its employees are a critical determinant for all career seekers. Similar majorities of heterosexual adults (86 percent) and gay, lesbian, bisexual, and transgender (GLBT) adults (90 percent) said they consider a company's employee benefits to be an important factor when choosing to work for one company over another. In addition, 79 percent of heterosexuals said it is important that their employer offers equal health insurance benefits to all employees.

The survey also disclosed an intriguing trend about heterosexual attitudes which suggest they increasingly consider diversity to be an important factor in deciding where to work. All other considerations being equal, the survey revealed that 73 percent of heterosexual adults consider it important that a company have a written nondiscrimination policy that includes sexual orientation in addition to race, ethnicity, sex, religion, age, and disability, compared to 63 percent of heterosexuals in 2002. In addition, 65 percent of heterosexual adults consider it important that a company promote and professionally develop senior managers who come from diverse backgrounds, compared to 56 percent in 2002.

These findings validate that workplace diversity is an important factor in helping establish the reputation of a company as well as how the marketplace and media tend to evaluate leadership in this area.

In our next chapter, we will focus on other unique attributes strongly linked to gay consumers, such as their very early and strong commitment to online media, as well as the attention they deserve as early adopters and trendsetters. We will also investigate the degree of influence that consumer knowledge and tailored advertising appear to play in lesbian and gay households.

CHAPTER 7

Gay Media, Connections, and Community

We often describe gays and lesbians as wary when it comes to public acceptance and social recognition. Given the palpable sense of stigma and fear of rejection that they have faced in American society over the years, it makes sense that trust looms so large for gay consumers.

These are deep-seated feelings that consistently shape how they perceive corporate, personal, and social behaviors. They tend to remain sensitive to how they are treated, how their relationships are respected, how they are wooed and won, and how they calibrate their expectations from an advertiser.

For many, they share an unquenchable human desire simply to be included on the same terms as everyone else. This has significant market implications that companies are beginning to understand and to which they are starting to respond.

This somewhat protective characteristic also helps explain, in part, why the GLBT population may be so information-hungry, why they crave media that speaks directly to them, and why they maintain a strong need for community—or strength in numbers.

Gays and lesbians, we witness, habitually seek to avoid isolation and wish to establish intimate relationships and foster their own sense of "chosen family" ties that include their closest friends and loved ones (particularly when they feel rejected or misunderstood by their own families).

The prevailing social silence and market vacuum in years past made it challenging if not impossible for many gays and lesbians to easily reach one another or to find gay-friendly venues and options—without resorting exclusively to their own codes and their own private channels, bookstores, bars and clubs, publications, language, relationships, and customs.

While all of these more conventional yet somewhat private channels provided legitimacy and social acceptance for gays and lesbians then, and still do have significant value, they also remained largely limited to major metropolitan areas, and are rarely found in smaller towns and rural areas. For many who remain in the closet for personal, family, or professional reasons, even these venues may seem far too risky to venture their faces and true names.

For marketers, these attitudes and consumer behaviors are especially challenging. How can a marketer reach consumers who not only find it hard to trust an advertiser but also are truly hard to find?

In the 1990s, with the rise of the Internet, of course, the sense of social isolation and alienation has changed forever as we briefly recounted in Chapter 2. This tide benefits customers and corporations alike. The frustrating boundaries of fleeting gay connections and possibilities were blown apart once same-sex feelings and attractions, aspirations, and needs discovered the safety and awesome virtual reach of the World Wide Web. Though a relatively small percentage of the world's overall population, GLBT people took to the Internet by storm to find friends, seek love and intimacy, consider commercial offers, and strengthen social bonds.

THE NEED TO CONNECT

While many Americans recognize the Internet only as an advanced tool for communications and productivity, gay Americans see it also as their personal and daily lifeline. For the first time ever, GLBT people had an extraordinary and safely anonymous cyber link to their counterparts around the block and around the world. They were able to connect in an instant with people who shared their fears and hopes, as well as their often misunderstood or mislabeled same-sex attraction.

Just as important, they were able to explore, build, and maintain an early and major presence on the Web that translates directly into tremendous market opportunities. In our research over the past few years, it is no surprise to discover consistently that gays and lesbians were among the first to explore the Internet, as well as to become frequent and heavy users of e-mail, chat rooms, and e-commerce. In almost every online behavior, we see that GLBT people overindex through their familiar habits, curiosity, and ultimately trust of familiar Web sites, chat rooms, and e-mail communications.

In addition to our own research findings, in 2003 Forrester Research Inc. ("Gays Are the Technology Early Adopters You Want") similarly reported that gay men and lesbians are more likely to be online. It reported that 80 percent of gay men and 76 percent of lesbians are Internet users, while only 70 percent of heterosexual men and 69 percent of heterosexual women are online. Substantially more gays (29 percent versus 18 percent) are long-time veterans of the Internet (in other words, they have been online for more than seven years). Since then, the true numbers have only grown.

GAY CONSUMERS HAVE STRONG NET BEHAVIORS

Compared to other, more conventional channels for information and resources, gay men and lesbians today appear more likely to turn to the Internet when they want to learn about a product or service. In our recent investigations, we find that the Internet is more likely to be used as a source of consumer information for GLBT consumers (33 percent) than word-of-mouth (31 percent) and consumer information organizations (22 percent).

Expanding on what previous Harris Interactive studies have shown about GLBT Internet use, in a March 2005 survey we also learned that two-thirds (66 percent) of gay adults frequently or occasionally visit mainstream online channels, compared with 57 percent of heterosexual adults. Gays also read Web logs (or "blogs") more often than their nongay counterparts (27 percent of gay adults frequently or occasionally seek out blogger Web sites versus 18 percent of heterosexual adults).

Gay and lesbian consumers clearly are more likely to use the Internet for news and information and political news and updates. They are, however, less likely to turn to the Internet for hobbies, games, and entertainment than their straight counterparts. In this sense, it appears that gay men and lesbians view the Internet more as a practical tool and a social net than a source of entertainment.

For shopping needs of all kinds—and more important, for actual purchasing—gays and lesbians are emboldened and eager. Witeck-Combs/Harris Interactive 2004 survey results show that GLBT consumers are more willing to use the Internet to make purchases too. This is consistent with the findings of the July 2003 Forrester Research Inc. report, which found that 63 percent of gay consumers surveyed indeed had made a purchase online, compared to just 53 percent of heterosexual online consumers. Since 2003, of course, these proportions continue to grow.

We also learned from this same research, not surprisingly, that in addition to seeking information, online advertising appears to have a stronger impact on gays. While only 35 percent of heterosexual consumers say that online advertisements influence their purchasing decisions, 42 percent of gay and lesbian consumers say they are influenced by online advertisements—particularly when the message or images are specifically tailored to them.

MEDIA HUNGRY AND SAVVY

Given the popularity of the Web among gays and lesbians and their strong behavioral ties to the Internet, the GLBT community has dedicated considerable ingenuity and talent to building online resources of all kinds.

Again and again, we see gays and lesbians as particularly early technology adopters—from digital photography and all forms of electronic music and video to creating and expanding original and popular Web destinations. Among the best-known Web sites are PlanetOut.com and Gay.com, which sprang from two related Internet channels that were popularly traveled by GLBT visitors. Gay.com began much as an online bulletin board or message board that permitted gays to communicate in a more static fashion by writing notes and ideas to each other, and then waiting for responses from each other.

PlanetOut.com originally was launched in two online platforms; first, as a dedicated GLBT-friendly space on the roller-coaster wings of America Online and then as a separate, integrated Web site with rich content and the same brand identity. Later, PlanetOut.com departed its home on AOL and soared on its own. PlanetOut.com and Gay.com as well as a number of other popular magnet sites quickly achieved strong chemistry with gays and lesbians by offering real-time chat as well as message boards, news, gossip, film reviews, personal ads, and, for the first time, online advertising creatively tailored to the gay consumer that attracted mainstream corporate brands.

The two sites—which currently attract millions of unique visitors and registered users each month—were combined under one company, PlanetOut, Inc. Together they made history by becoming the first valuable global media property owned and managed primarily by a GLBT corporate team to be publicly traded on Nasdaq in 2004. Even after the collapse of technology stocks and the deflated Internet bubble in 2000, the PlanetOut culture, community, and enterprise continued to expand, add more revenue-generating sales features, and, most of all, remain profitable despite the stock market doldrums that immediately followed.

Other Internet media in the GLBT community thrive as well, such as Hyperion Interactive Media (recently purchased by Here!

Television), which aggregated many of its own and several independent sites to create a multimillion-customer pool of varied and popular GLBT content Web sites. AfterEllen, Gay Financial Network, LesbiaNation, LesbianAlliance, 365 gay Outsports, Women in the Life (designed for lesbians of color), and Gaywheels are several Web sites that tailored their relevant content and audience mix for men, women, people of color, sports enthusiasts, and others to provide social connections, information, news, and commerce.

Social online networks such as Friendster, while not designed uniquely for GLBT users, clearly have achieved strong resonance within the gay community. Later incarnations such as myspace .com also seem to bring a cutting-edge appeal to draw connection-hungry, younger lesbians and gay men too. Feeding these strong needs for virtual community combined with social change has also become the mission of Tim Gill, the talented software entrepreneur and philanthropist, who heads the Gill Foundation in Colorado. In 2003, he launched one of the newest online channels, Connexion.org, as a virtual meeting space for GLBT people who share his equality-minded beliefs for American political progress.

PRINT RULES TOO

Long before the Web rocked the world for millions of gays and lesbians, the power of print played a leading role that has never diminished over the years.

Since the 1950s, gay and lesbian magazines, newspapers, newsletters, and tabloids have emerged, grown, and often withstood an onslaught of legal, political, economic, and cultural challenges. They also have struggled with ways to attract advertisers that were sensitive about the publications' questionable content and their acceptance of explicit gay personal ads.

It has taken a generation or two of America's most formidable gay visionaries to proudly write, publish, and profitably circulate publications for their community. In a tough business, many have failed along the way. Yet many more continue to seek, serve, and grow their loyal readerships.

From the 1980s and 1990s forward, gay entrepreneurs led by pioneering LPI Publications (purchased in 2005 by PlanetOut, Inc.) and its flagship magazines, the *Advocate* and *Out*, began to retool their editorial content and marketability. Leading gay newspapers also followed suit and transformed their presence to attract more readers and lure valuable local ad sales.

All have done so by focusing far more editorial attention on entertainment, lifestyle, apparel, travel, and home furnishings as a way to bridge the strong interests of readers with the desire of companies to speak directly to their customers through their pages. While remaining true to their audiences' diverse tastes and needs, they also flung open wide a door to mainstream companies that understand the value and potential of the gay consumer—such as film studios, alcohol producers, apparel manufacturers, pharmaceutical companies, hospitality services, financial institutions, automotive companies, and the makers of personal care products, to highlight a few.

Today there is a broader range of general interest magazines, yet most titles still appear to remain targeted to predominantly white, disproportionately younger, upscale, and urban gay men. Prominent national women's titles, however, include *Curve* and *Velvetpark*. In 2005, gay African-Americans also found a new possibility in *Nyansapo*, published by the National Black Justice Coalition.

Newer national titles in the past few years include *MetroSource, Genre, Instinct, Scene,* and *Pink*; as well as specialized publications for Web enthusiasts, such as *Gay Web Monkey*; for same-sex parents, such as *Proud Parenting*; for gay ideas and scholarship, such as *The Gay and Lesbian Review*; for lesbian and gay travelers, such as *Out Traveller, Out & About,* and *Passport*; and for gay youth, such as *YGA* and *Xodus*.

Given the growing options available within gay media, we wanted to learn more about media consumption as well. How do gays and lesbians respond to all forms of media?

In a study we conducted three years ago with Harris Interactive, we asked about readership patterns for national gay magazines, such as *The Advocate, Out,* and *Curve.* One-third (34 percent) of respondents say they read these publications frequently or occasionally. However, when also asked about news sources that allow for somewhat greater anonymity, such as online channels like Gay.com and PlanetOut.com, not surprisingly, over four in ten (41 percent) GLBT individuals surveyed frequently or occasionally visit gay online channels. One in five (19 percent) GLBT respondents also reported they frequently or occasionally read their local gay newspaper. (This figure may appear deceivingly low but many gays and lesbians regrettably do not live in communities that write and distribute a local gay publication.)

What more can we learn about these media consumers?

Fortunately, in early 2005, a timely study was released by the National Gay Newspaper Guild (NGNG), the professional association of leading gay newspapers in the United States, which includes member newspapers in San Francisco, Boston, Detroit, Dallas, Los Angeles, San Diego, Houston, New York, Philadelphia, Atlanta, Washington, D.C., Miami, and Chicago. It gathered samples of over 3,800 adults (age 18 and over) who are readers of an NGNG publication and a separate general sample of 2,731 U.S. adults (age 18 and over).

Gays and lesbians who read the nation's top gay newspapers were found to have a range of compelling traits. They were found to be more socially outgoing, to travel more frequently, and to be more concerned about health and fitness than the general U.S. adult population.

On education and earnings, the survey found even more distinctions. The sampled gay readers had more than twice as many college degrees as the average U.S. adult population (67 percent vs. 25 percent) with the graduating class earning more than three times as many graduate degrees (28 percent vs. 8 percent).

FIGURE 7.1 National Gay Newspaper Guild ad

Source: National Gay Newspaper Guild. Used with permission.

These readers tended to have higher personal and household incomes and higher household net worth than the average U.S. adult population.

How have advertisers responded? In the past few years, advertising executive Howard Buford, CEO of Prime Access, one of the nation's leading multicultural advertising agencies, in partnership with Todd Evans of Rivendell Media, a respected broker for advertisers seeking gay media, examined the overall metrics of America's gay media and its dynamic advertising base. Their market investigations produced valuable findings.

In 2005, as they have done for over a decade, they analyzed the top 139 news and entertainment titles among the four kinds of publications serving gay readers in America today—from local magazines, newspapers, and entertainment guides to national magazines and one national newspaper, *The Lesbian News.*

Their 2005 *Gay Press Report* suggests that the combined U.S. readership for these 151 top publications is no fewer than 3.4 million people. (The total universe of gay print media can be estimated to include between 200 and 250 separate titles, though quite a few have limited or no advertising and others are not audited or generally available through commercial distribution or newsstands. Many also are distributed in less conventional fashion primarily through gay neighborhoods, bars, bookstores, and community centers, as well as through the mail.)

With total advertising revenues as the barometer, the trends are very promising. For the key publications studied, they found that $212 million in sales was generated in 2005, an increase of 189 percent since 1996. Just as fascinating, they learned that over 175 Fortune 500 brands had advertised that year in the gay media (up from 72 in 2001 and a meager 19 major U.S. brands in 1994).

These findings underscore the true metrics of gay market growth and maturity, and the still unmet desires for Madison Avenue to bridge more and more gay households. In the past decade, since 1996, gay media ad revenues in print alone are estimated to have soared over 200 percent. If we include online advertising, which has not yet been measured in the same fashion, the favorable trends would be even clearer.

BEYOND GAY MEDIA

Lesbians and gay men, as well as bisexual and transgender adults, are avid consumers of media beyond the gay community. Again and again, we find evidence that gay consumers are more likely than others to seek and find information, resources, entertainment, and enterprise in all forms of media, including many mainstream outlets.

In June 2003, we undertook a comprehensive online consumer research study of GLBT consumers and nongay adults, testing an overall panel of nearly 2,400 adults. In general, we found GLBT consumers tend to read and view many of the same forms of media as their heterosexual counterparts. However, across the board, gay adults tended to favor lifestyle, home decorating, and design magazines; news magazines; and premium cable networks more than their nongay counterparts.

We discovered that 60 percent of the GLBT individuals queried said they frequently or occasionally read mainstream news magazines, such as *Time* and *Newsweek*; the same is true of only 45 percent of heterosexuals surveyed. In addition, 41 percent of gay consumers say they read lifestyle, home decorating, and design magazines, such as *Martha Stewart Living* or *Architectural Digest*, frequently or occasionally, compared with 30 percent of nongay respondents.

In March 2005, we confirmed many of our original findings about gay media consumption, and also focused more scrutiny on cable television networks and alternative forms of media. In an overall national sample exceeding 2,600 adults, we found that three-quarters (76 percent) of the gay respondents frequently or occasionally watch basic cable, compared with two-thirds (67 percent) of heterosexual adults. Similarly, six in ten (62 percent) gay respondents reported they frequently or occasionally watch specialty cable networks, compared with 56 percent of heterosexuals; and 45 percent report they frequently or occasionally watch premium (pay) cable networks, compared with 37 percent of heterosexuals.

This study also highlighted strong preferences toward reading alternative newspapers among GLBT adults. While one-half (49 percent) of gay respondents state they frequently or occasionally read the alternative press, only one-quarter (27 percent) of heterosexual adults say they do. Likewise, three in ten (31 percent) gay respondents say they frequently or occasionally listen to independent and alternative radio stations, compared with one-quarter (25 percent) of nongay respondents.

Gays and lesbians are as avid as ever about connecting to television programming and publications that are directly relevant to their lives, needs, and tastes.

EMERGENCE OF GAY TELEVISION NETWORKS

In a nation with almost as many television sets today as pairs of eyeballs, it is fitting to celebrate the love affair that gay and lesbian Americans have long had with television too. Our research underscores that avid gay consumers overindex in their cable television subscription and viewing habits, particularly when it comes to special and premium networks. They are accustomed to looking at all kinds of channels and specialized programming to find glimpses of their lives and relationships.

For over two decades, television trends have often broken with convention and have boldly added original gay themes, stories, characters, and issues to their daily lineup. Despite these unmistakable signs of inclusion and visibility, however, prior to 2004 there had never been a channel dedicated primarily to gays and lesbians. What has changed today?

Very simply, given the expanded digital spectrum available now through cable, satellite, and telecom delivery, as well as the changing habits of next generation viewers and the evolutionary segmenting of television tastes, specialized niche programming has become a reality and not just a promise. In the 1960s, three national broadcasting networks seemed to satisfy most Americans. Fifty years later, it seems we can hardly live without 300 channels and more.

Given the booming digital spectrum, why not create and drive cable entertainment networks for sports fans, women, gamblers, pet owners, teens, home decorators, food fanatics, small kids, communities of faith, Latinos, African-Americans, car nuts, comedy lovers, and travelers? Television advertisers now are presented with stunning menus, possibilities, and options for how they choose to spotlight and speak to their distinct audiences, including gays and lesbians and their families and friends.

Students of pop culture appreciate that risk-taking producers basked in the acceptance of sitcoms such as *Soap* that made Billy Crystal a star in the 1970s as one of the first gay characters of an ensemble show. Crystal, of course, has long been joined by countless other gay characters in guest performances and supporting roles on some of America's most popular series, films, and reality shows.

In addition, for more than a decade, a smartly produced and seasoned gay news magazine show, *In The Life*, has long been available through syndication on a supportive network of local PBS stations that tend to air the format late in the evening. Public access channels also have fostered community-based gay programming developed by volunteers and activists. These efforts have earned very loyal yet limited audiences, and succeeded most often on a shoestring, yet have never been able to achieve commercial breakthroughs.

In 1997, Ellen DeGeneres's spectacular "coming out" on television as well as in her own life presented a cultural sea change and an unforgettable moment in television broadcast history. It was certainly a moment that few if any gay Americans will forget. Her original comedy series regrettably was caught in a tailspin of declining ratings, yet her subsequent successful trajectory as an openly gay performer has been almost as breathtaking. She retrieved her strong ratings and earned accolades later as a popular host of the Emmy Awards and by excelling as the host of her own daytime talk show.

Surfing on Ellen's wave also made possible the introduction of two other brazenly gay and amazingly popular programs—the NBC comedy series, *Will & Grace*, and Bravo's unique makeover show, *Queer Eye for the Straight Guy*. Both casts played largely for boundless laughs as well as stereotypes. Fortunately, they also reflected a strong crossover appeal with all audiences, especially straight women who make up a solid segment of the television viewing audience today.

Nielsen data published in *Broadcasting & Cable* (May 3, 2004) tested the popularity of these programs. *Will & Grace* and *Queer Eye for the Straight Guy* earned higher than average marks across America's midsection. For example, *Will & Grace* earned a Nielsen rating in Peoria, Illinois, that is 20 percent higher than the national average. *It's Relative*, a comedy that featured two gay parents (though short-lived, it is now shown in syndication on

Logo) generated ratings substantially stronger in Louisville, Kentucky (63 percent above average); Nashville, Tennessee (57 percent); Oklahoma City, Oklahoma (14 percent); Richmond, Virginia (30 percent); and Kansas City, Missouri (20 percent). *The L Word*, a popular lesbian ensemble series on Showtime, attracts six times its average audience in Birmingham, Alabama, while in Salt Lake City, its audience is eight times larger than the national average.

The most important lesson of all was simple: the advertisers, as a rule, did not flee, hide nor shrink from these programs. They discovered that the acid tests were not gay actors, gay characters, or gay plot lines. The true test for success was audience appeal and acceptance. No doubt they braced for the very worst that might happen. They were more than pleasantly surprised that quality and originality had universal appeal that trumped hostility or fears. Television is a powerful way to test-drive ideas and these were two ideas that paved the way for what was soon to follow.

Beginning in 2004, it seems many prayers were finally answered when not one but three specialized cable television networks were launched and intended primarily for the GLBT market. In fact, we served as consulting communications experts for MTV Networks to help bring Logo to the marketplace in June 2005. Logo was created as the first 24/7 advertising-supported digital cable network—joining two subscription-based premium services called Here! and Q Television that aired live just months before. (As we write this, however, Q Television has collapsed, likely the result of its fragile financial footing from the outset.)

The fledgling networks arrived on America's doorstep with much promise, as well as keen ambitions to be discovered and warmly embraced by the GLBT community (and with luck, some crossover appeal). All three had to make convincing business cases to cable and satellite operators to navigate their way onto America's television sets, and Logo had the added sales goal of bringing more than 50 mainstream advertisers on air in its first year to provide commercial sponsorships for their gay-

FIGURE 7.2 Logo ad

Source: LOGO. Used with permission.

themed films, news, music, comedy, documentaries, and original series.

Remarkably, all achieved generous distribution within America's multi-million household universe of digital cable. When combined with satellite penetration as well, gay networks and loyal viewers today may be found in all 50 states. In its first six months, Logo aimed high by seeking distribution in no fewer than ten million households; yet the network not only met its original lofty goal, but nearly doubled it by the end of 2005 while adding a prestigious roster of advertisers, such as car makers, pharmaceutical companies, wireless service providers, beverage manufacturers, hospitality services, and film companies among others.

BACK TO THE FUTURE WITH RADIO

While the advanced digital spectrum promised us new gay cable television networks, it also has made possible the growing programming spectrum on satellite radio networks XM and Sirius. If targeted television networks make sense, why not digital radio networks with hundreds of channels delivering talk, news, entertainment, and all forms of music? Why not a gay radio network too?

Of course, gay talk radio has long been a local fixture in many urban markets for years including popular programs in San Francisco, Minneapolis, Austin, Los Angeles, Chicago, Boston, and numerous other smaller markets. These formats often are found on university campuses and at public radio stations, which do not ordinarily seek advertising support. However, others are found operating in commercial space on the FM spectrum.

In the spring of 2003, Sirius followed through with the creation of the first national gay radio network. It invested in the creation of a full slate of sponsor-supported radio shows for GLBT and GLBT-friendly listeners called OutQ Radio, conceived by veteran radio entrepreneur John McMullen. McMullen had long sought to combine forces nationally with other journalists to present an attractive menu of gay-centric news, talk, and entertainment and make it available across America in subscriber homes, workplaces, and cars around the clock.

While OutQ thrives, in early 2006, it was joined on the radio dial by a newcomer called Twist. Logo founder and entertainment executive Matt Farber launched Twist, a nationally syndicated radio brand beginning with a weekly two-hour show called "Radio with a Twist" to feature celebrity interviews, music, and entertainment reports along with news and relationship advice. The syndicated programming almost immediately found its way to major FM stations in nine leading cities including Los Angeles, New York, San Francisco, and Atlanta, as well as on the Internet through AOL Radio distribution.

In very tangible ways, lesbians and gays are more enthusiastic than ever to discover common ground, find knowledge, be entertained, make purchases, and find one-on-one connections through all forms of powerful media. And for marketers, the expanding opportunities to reach their customers and bridge to these gay households have never been stronger.

In Part Three, we will share the practical experience we have acquired over more than a decade helping corporate America engineer these bridges while planning prudently for discomfort and occasions of cultural backlash.

The Strategy

CHAPTER 8

Steps for Success

Strategies in the Real World

We are dogged about preparation when it comes to sustaining winning strategies for the buying power of the gay consumer market, estimated to be $641 billion in 2006. Any effective market strategy demands discipline. Given the understandable complexities and growing visibility of gay America, this is even truer.

Positioning a campaign for success follows our hands-on experiences with many companies over the past decade. We will highlight corporate examples here to give future marketers confidence to execute their business plans too.

For the purpose of safeguarding client confidences, however, we also have taken care not to disclose proprietary details. Nonetheless, any marketer will benefit from this experience as well as our seasoned tips on avoiding pitfalls. Here are seven steps to successful strategies for the GLBT marketplace today.

STEP 1: LOOK INSIDE

Market readiness can take on many meanings for a company. It may mean the design, engineering, and manufacturing lifecycle of a product, or perhaps the skills of packagers, media planners, copywriters, and marketing specialists who choose where, when, and how to connect with their intended audience.

In designing a strategy for the gay community, we first probe the company's philosophy, policies, and relationship with its own employees. As we described earlier, gay consumers approach a company without blinders. They frequently judge whether the brand is indeed welcoming, fair-minded, and respectful; therefore, internal education is a must.

Other consumer groups make this step plain too. African-Americans and Hispanics, likewise, sense when a company's reputation for inclusion is real or simply lip service, and whether the company has in place the cultural sensitivity and authentic outreach that resonates with them.

In recent years, some restaurant franchises, retail stores, and hotel chains have learned hard lessons about untrained and uneven customer service in serving people of color. Missteps and poor training are not uncommon in the treatment of customers living with disabilities either. Rebuilding reputation following these wayward instances can be tough because customers often see past mere words and a few actions to detect whether a company has a genuine commitment.

For gays, lesbians, bisexuals, and transgender people, the logical sensitivities also extend to how the company treats its own employees and not just its customers. As our research highlights, gay customers increasingly favor companies that understand and treat their own gay employees and honor their committed relationships in fair and even-handed ways. There is no aim for gays and lesbians to achieve special, preferred, or favored treatment, but simply to apply the same standards and expectations as all other workers. Repeated surveys over the past few years show two-thirds of all Americans agree, and favor equitable workplace treatment. Most seem to see this as equal pay for equal work and a simple matter of fairness.

Gay consumers also see that a company's policies present a reasonable mirror on how they as customers are likely to be treated too. If a company is silent and has no meaningful policies that reflect sexual orientation, gays presume the company will remain invisible at best.

Gay consumers know from experience that companies willing to search their soul and invest the time, patience, and care to advance their corporate culture, adopt policies of nondiscrimination and equal benefits, and become engaged in the gay community are true brand leaders. They tend to rank these companies high when making comparative choices, particularly when other factors such as price, quality, function, and convenience are reasonably competitive. We have seen evidence that gay consumers are even willing to pay a slight premium to patronize a company whose principles and reputation are convincingly known to be strong.

We sometimes call this internal education a *360-degree philosophy,* and recommend companies think in that fashion. Internal education makes sense by including all divisions of management, and not simply the niche marketing team.

The reason? Gay and lesbian marketing touches every part of a company. When companies think that they can pursue the market in a vacuum, avoidable problems most often arise.

Year in and year out, we help advise human resource managers, legal counsel, public affairs managers, corporate communications professionals, and marketing executives how their overall corporate position influences hard-won perceptions about their brand and their company. Missteps in applying rules for domestic partners, for example, or a regrettably poor choice of words hurriedly spoken when a boycott is threatened can drive wedges between the company and gay households.

Typically, when beginning to work with a company, we conduct an overall gay market assessment that starts with basics—the company's mission statement, its own character, and its EEO policies and practices—to check whether they include protections against discrimination for sexual orientation and gender identity. While an overwhelming number of Fortune 500 companies today explicitly include sexual orientation policies, many still do not yet protect gender identity or expression. This trend, however, is picking up and more diversity officers and human resource educators are becoming familiar with the importance of including all.

We then review whether benefits for same-sex partners are extended equal to those given married partners; whether the company offers a diversity training curriculum that includes sexual orientation (along with race, ethnicity, and other characteristics); and whether it sponsors employee resource networks or employee groups that represent GLBT co-workers. Giving gay employees an equal voice in the company's culture is a strong tool to promote loyalty, develop common values among all employees, and deliver on promises to treat all equally.

Corporate citizenship is also an area that deserves attention. Most major companies today declare their community ties and philanthropy by giving back a share of their returns to nonprofits and community groups important to their employees. Typically, this includes varied beneficiaries such as hospitals, education programs, inspiring causes, and well-respected charities. Whether cause-related marketing or direct contributions, each of these sponsorships plays a role in defining the company's core values. When a company overlooks or simply neglects causes that are meaningful to a portion of its community or its employee base, it is almost always noticed. Giving to gay-related causes is a sign of unmistakable good will, and quite often part of an overall marketing strategy.

For gays and lesbians, this has taken on larger relevance in the past decade. Today, more companies realize that contributing to AIDS charities, for example, which still need generous support, is not the only way to support the GLBT community. Instead, they now expand their outreach to various gay nonprofits, urban community centers, lesbian cancer and health centers, scholarships for gay students, and other forms of tangible generosity reflecting the community's needs. Companies also align with prominent gay civil rights causes as a specialized form of cause-related marketing through mutual values.

We finally consider whether a company has earned awards, honors, or special recognition from the GLBT community along the way, or gathered attention and support for its fair-minded and inclusive approach to doing business. On the flip side, we also inquire whether the company has an indefensible track record of troubling litigation or disquieting claims of discriminatory treatment of its gay and lesbian employees. If so, we try to determine if there are patterns that require attention and remedy.

Sometimes it comes down to internal training as well. Following the tragic events of September 11, for example, we helped advise a major hospitality company about unforeseen issues surrounding the heightened scrutiny given to travelers passing through airports and checkpoints. It may seem a slight challenge to most of us, but consider the vulnerability of a transgender woman alone and on business. If your government-issued identity card and photograph no longer matches your current appearance, then you may find yourself in a security screening catch-22 and more likely to miss a crucial flight or travel connection.

A small snafu that distorts lawful identity also may arise when a gay male couple simply travels with their young child. They might also be detained, questioned, or profiled, because, to some security-sensitive officials, they may not appear to be the child's lawful parents. In many scenarios today, airlines and other travel leaders have enhanced obligations to help all their customers travel with dignity, comfort, and support. For gays and lesbians, and for transgender people, the gaps in law, custom, and procedure can present hurdles that smart companies try to ease. Through internal education and training that recognizes the diverse needs of all customers, these missteps are fewer and not so costly to a company's reputation.   .

For good and bad, and as a focus of internal education, we try to understand how a company speaks inside its own walls before it takes its message outside to its customers. This is the true basis of bringing business "inside out" and establishing a lasting reputation in the market.

STEP 2: LOOK OUTSIDE

When we complete the internal review and our first focus on corporate education, we also try to paint a clear picture of where the company stands in the market itself. We throw a spotlight on how the company stacks up among its rivals, and also within corporate America generally. Is it a leader or follower in the pack? What does it mean to be a leader? How does it establish its credentials?

Many sectors today are hotly competitive. We see advanced fields of technology as well as older industrial sectors, such as the automobile industry and airlines, as obvious examples. For different reasons, but with the same businesslike motivation, all of these players are struggling to stay ahead of their competitors, advance their best products and services, hire and retain the strongest talents, and deliver strong steady profits to their investors.

It's no wonder these are industries in which competition for the best employees and share of the gay wallet really matter. This also is true in an aggressive arena such as financial services, where we try to understand what all the top players are doing.

We start by asking and investigating. For instance, which banks and brokerages advertise in gay media, and how much are they spending? Are they using general market creative, or applying gay-specific messaging, images, and sensibilities to their execution? What products are they championing? What does their messaging say, and to whom are they saying it? Where is their brand best known in the gay community? Are they conducting integrated marketing in many channels, or just a handful? Do they sponsor gay nonprofits and community causes? Which companies have earned the strongest reputation among gay consumers, and why? How a company approaches its advertising speaks volumes about the depth of its understanding and commitment to the market.

All of these questions matter. They echo the same ones we ask each company to mine its experience, learn what it has tried, and see what kinds of preliminary marketing it has tested. In many cases, this attention to detail provides us a clearer snapshot of the competitive environment and the starting point for all future efforts.

STEP 3: FOCUS ON RESEARCH

With our seasoned commitment to applied research and some of the best tools available, we believe, as most marketers do, that it is the foundation for almost all marketing strategies. With our partner, Harris Interactive, we have made smart investments in developing research-based plans for automakers, media and entertainment companies, think tanks, information technology leaders, and wireless companies.

Where does research lead us? For a start, it enables us to avoid untested assumptions or plain guesswork. Instead, we have the ability to offer companies greater confidence to:

- *Screen GLBT online panelists to ensure they are qualified users of the products or services we test.* When studying alcoholic beverages, for instance, we determine whether the test participants actually buy and drink them. When we explore the brand equity of automobiles, we first make sure that the gay respondents in fact are licensed drivers who have personal experience with car selections, sales, and leases.

- *Segment GLBT consumers better to learn whether there are identifiable age, income, race, gender disparities, or other unique traits that suggest differences in the individual's affinity toward a product or a brand.* Do gay men or lesbians have stronger interest in imports, or for environmentally friendly automobiles? With lesbians more likely to parent than gay men, what automotive models address their families' needs best? We can never assume that all GLBT consumers are alike or that they behave monolithically. Research enables us to learn the behavioral similarities and differences among different segments of the population.

- *Contrast distinctions, where they are found to exist, between gay households and nongay households.* When testing consumption, brand consideration, and brand equity, we try to discover whether or not gay consumers are truly less price-sensitive or more label-conscious than their straight neighbors and friends, especially when testing Web usage, measuring the frequency of cell phone upgrades, or choosing among a broad selection of digital cameras, for example.

■ *Discover the hot buttons and resonant messages for gay consumers that lead them to make clear preferences.* What influences affect GLBT consumers when ordering or serving alcoholic beverages or choosing vacation destinations, for example?

■ *Test print and broadcast advertising concepts with gay and nongay audiences to find what connects best with target gay buyers, without alienating a nongay consumer with the same advertising image.*

Over ten years ago, before the Internet suggested cost-effective innovations, most forms of conventional market research were more costly and complex, particularly for testing harder-to-find populations like gays and lesbians. In campaign mode now, however, online research provides essential tools to conceive, tailor, and execute effective marketing approaches. Research also permits us to measure actual awareness and consideration by establishing an initial baseline before launch, as well as post-campaign surveys to determine whether the desirable impressions and responses are reached.

STEP 4: AVOID PARTIAL COMMITMENTS AND OVERBLOWN EXPECTATIONS

Time and again, we see curious instances where marketers experiment with a single advertisement, or perhaps a solitary direct mail pitch. These one-trick strategies guess that a calculated pass at the market will reach and resonate with a broad cross-section of promising, affluent gay households.

To their surprise and frequent disappointment, more often than not, they find themselves puzzled with the lackluster performance in a limited overture. Some seem to surrender their original ambitions, or at least mortgage their assumptions about the promised hyper-responsiveness of gay households. Common sense goes out the window when the gay market is imagined as a springboard to rewards with little exertion.

Seasoned and successful brands, on the other hand, understand these issues and take a pragmatic posture. They recognize that in order to effectively measure and grow outreach to this market, a legitimate investment of time, resources, and educated management commitment is required. One of the most common reasons for GLBT marketing efforts to be curtailed in their effectiveness appears to come from sacrificing time and planning, and delivering inadequate resources across the board. Would any other niche market respond differently to a new entrant or novel one-shot campaign?

Niche marketing does not insist that we abandon logic or conventional marketing wisdom. To introduce, woo, and win all new customers, effective marketing strategies frequently rely on multiple and integrated layers that frequently require months to reach desirable penetration. When you combine tested advertising with customer education and nonprofit sponsorships, it is more likely to cement a proper foundation to then reap the benefits. To get GLBT consumers to recognize and trust a gay-friendly appeal, and to establish trust with a brand, is a long journey, not an overnight trip.

Yet, for a market that compares favorably in buying power and consumer traits with other niche markets, it is surprising how often companies that have felt effective in the GLBT market tend to make basic business decisions *differently* than they do in other categories.

Sound marketing decisions also are based on data that supports the historical experiences a company has had with its products and services in other markets, such as the features and functions that sell and why, the demographic characteristics that define strong customer prospects; the tried-and-true channels for serving other consumer segments (advertising, direct mail), and so on.

STEP 5: GET THE MESSAGE AND IMAGES RIGHT

When speaking to most customers, marketers benefit from years of creative trial and error as well as costly investments in mountains of psychographic data to help them probe the interior of America's households. They want to know what moves the dial and makes a sale possible.

Yet, as society has evolved and America reflects a richer diversity of households, cultures, languages, and ethnic identities, the sophisticated advertiser understands that it takes keener perception and insight to target the minds and wallets of prospective buyers and to really know them.

It has taken generations for Madison Avenue to meaningfully reflect and portray African-American images and voices, learn the varied Spanish-speaking byways, and discover the many Asian and Pacific Islander cultural nuances and preferences. We work today with progressive companies such as Verizon Wireless, for example, to help its marketers communicate persuasively and sensitively to connect with customers living with disabilities. Knowing your customer is Marketing 101, and that must be underscored even more for gays, lesbians, bisexual, and transgender Americans.

Diversity in attitude, messaging, and execution makes a difference in the gay consumer market. Often advertisers are questioned, challenged, or criticized if their take is exclusively monochromatic and overemphasizes the obvious. So much of the media and marketplace today continues to magnify the hip, young, gay, white urban male, and tends to overlook so much of the richness that makes up the GLBT universe.

There are changes underway, fortunately. We see keener acknowledgement of these characteristics, and we see firsthand the evolution in the work of companies such as Prime Access, a leading multicultural advertising agency that reflects bolder hues, varied ethnic backgrounds, and sexual orientation in many corporate campaigns. In fact, we partnered with Prime Access over several years to engineer an award-winning automotive branding campaign for Volvo that highlights the visibility of "family" within gay households. Our images and messaging spoke to men and women, and the need many gays and lesbians feel to choose their families, find a loving life partner, and raise children much as everyone else does. Unlike almost all mainstream advertising today, the same-sex couples we presented included an interracial pair, which is more commonplace among same-sex households than conventional heterosexual couples. In Chapter 9, we will tell the full story of this innovative campaign.

One outstanding resource for advertisers may be found in the comprehensive commercial archive maintained online by the Commercial Closet Association, founded by veteran journalist Mike Wilke. We work closely with the Commercial Closet Association as friendly advisors and supporters. A trusted board of advertising, marketing, and media professionals on which Bob Witeck serves represents this nonprofit educational project.

The Commercial Closet Association (*www.commercialcloset.org*) does not browbeat or demand that marketers follow strict rules or simply pay lip service through politically correct notions of advertising. Instead, its overarching focus is on education and the use of practical and effective examples to show the market many possible ways to create inclusive mainstream and business-to-business advertising that is respectful of gay, lesbian, bisexual, and transgender people above all, while promoting creativity, sales, and image goals for the marketer.

Drawing on reporting observations, trial, experience, data, and analysis from industry leaders, the Commercial Closet Association has developed an excellent menu of *best practices* that we endorse *and* apply frequently to our own work. These tips are fully intended for mainstream advertising that speaks to all customers, yet we believe it offers valuable counsel for targeted campaigns that specifically address the GLBT market. A visit to the Commercial Closet Association Web site will reveal examples of *best practices* (and some of the worst), and we recommend all advertisers digest and consider their approaches along these lines:

- *Be inclusive and diverse.* Whenever people are shown in advertising, try to include GLBT individuals, family members, friends, or couples that reflect varied ages, races, and genders. Language references to family or relationships should not be hetero-centric but might refer instead to partners.

- *Avoid positioning homosexuality or gender identity as a perceived threat for humor.* This perspective recommends avoiding cheap jokes. Scenarios about cross-dressing or heterosexual fears about homosexual advances that play for laughs ought to be considered a thing of the past.

- *Be sensitive to gay, lesbian, bisexual, and transgender stereotypes.* Mike Wilke notes that advertising often stereotypes for impact, but beware of complications that turn off an audience. Feminine gay men and deceitful and scary transgender people are clichés that alienate many, and "lipstick lesbians" alone are limiting. He cautions to seek a fresh balance and unexpected twists by countering stereotypes and timeworn approaches.

- *Do good research.* We can't say it enough: When conducting general research or forming new mainstream campaigns, GLBT perspectives should be considered and included as often as possible.

- *Go national.* Consumers outside of major coast cities are often improperly considered lacking sophistication to handle GLBT themes in advertising. We've learned time and again that popular television series with gay stories, characters, and themes frequently seem to soar in unexpected places like Salt Lake City, Des Moines, and Kansas City.

- *Be consistent and confident.* After launching an ad campaign, stick with it. Modifying or withdrawing ads suggests waffling and creates potential trouble or unwanted media attention. Respond to any criticism with business rationales, with an emphasis on diversity and the bottom line. Avoid time-restricted airings of material unless ads legitimately deal with sexual situations inappropriate for young audiences.

See Appendix B for more expert and detailed discussion from the Commercial Closet Association about executing *best practices* in GLBT advertising.

STEP 6: KNOW THE GLBT COMMUNITY

Historically, African-Americans often find pride, strength, and comfort in familiar institutions, such as family and church, as well as barbershops and hair salons, for example. Similar observations might be drawn about Asian-Americans and Latinos who cherish their own family rituals, traditions, and venues. Knowing the code so often means knowing the culture, bonds, and language of a group. Recognizing the gathering places, byways, voices, and culture of a niche population allows marketers to recommend trusted channels that are known to connect.

For the GLBT community, there are similarities and differences. We see that gay people come from all walks of life, ethnic backgrounds, geographies, religious beliefs, and economic classes. In one sense they are a richly diverse group of people, with few apparent natural bonds or common traits apart from their identity and intimate attractions. The GLBT community is comprised of young, old, men, and women, of all races and experience, who as sexual minorities frequently are rejected, misunderstood, or simply set apart from society's overarching pressures to conform.

We often say that lesbians and gays choose their own families based on intimacy, trust, and deep friendship. They don't always sit down at their birth family's Thanksgiving table; instead, they are likely to create their own traditions and close gatherings. Finding lasting human attachments requires some ingenuity as well as conventional and nonconventional ways to raise children, establish families and domestic partnerships (having been denied marriage rights), and avoid alienation by creating real bonds of community.

Smart marketers get it. They recognize that a gay household may not always walk, talk, look, or act exactly like a conventional American family—even though, the truth be told, we've found there really is no such thing as a conventional American family. We are a nation of single and divorced parents, retirees, roommates, loving same-sex partners, and group homes, as well as the more fabled family model of two parents with kids.

Lesbians and gay men, moreover, have created a rich assortment of their own institutions to connect their needs and establish roots. When the mere act of dating and meeting others socially was necessary, they opened bars, clubs, and restaurants. When doctors responded curtly or negligently about their health status, especially at the height of the AIDS epidemic, the gay community established free health clinics and AIDS service organizations to rally around. When lesbians felt marginalized or isolated, they created bookshops and coffee houses for poetry slams and dating opportunities. When denied even welcome at their own churches, they founded new churches and places of worship. When one or more doors slammed in their faces, they opened new doors. Nothing could be more human or more understandable than for a stigmatized group to create its own safety, strength, and closeness.

Gay organizations and institutions today run the gamut; we already have highlighted the role of gay media channels. Within the community itself, there are boundless nonprofits that advocate civil rights, fairer laws, the needs of gay service members, people of faith, parents of gay kids, straight kids with gay parents, health advocates, and immigration reformers, just to name a few.

Gay organizations have launched a rich and sometimes dizzying assortment of GLBT-oriented chambers of commerce, film festivals, pride celebrations, rodeo groups, bowling and softball leagues, auto hobbyist clubs, writers groups, athletic associations, and political interests. To this day, they give strong evidence to Alexis de Tocqueville's observation that Americans are habitual joiners. Remaining alone is not our strong suit.

Effective marketing strategies recognize this penchant, and find meaningful ways to tap into the networks and institutions that gays and lesbians have established. Building bridges, establishing sponsorships, and supporting the volunteer services of clinics, sporting leagues, and entertainers is a sensitive way to truly be part of the community and grow market share.

It is more and more common for corporate brands to establish cause-related marketing approaches to tie their reputation to the causes and communities that are trusted by lesbians and gays.

Different approaches make sense for varied marketers. With popular automotive brands, for example, we created special incentive awards that targeted a portion of the sales price to two leading and nationally respected nonprofits, the Human Rights Campaign and the Gay & Lesbian Alliance Against Defamation. Prospective buyers understood through print, events, online promotions, and, eventually, word of mouth—as well as eager dealerships in several locales—that their purchase decisions benefited the community while delivering a stronger net return on sales and leases than originally imagined.

Many other brands have offered similar stakes by allocating a share of their profits to beneficiaries through foundations. For example, RSVP Travel, which is best known for its popular all-gay cruise adventures, provides generous assistance through its partnership with the Kevin Mossier Foundation. MBNA's multi-year relationship with the affinity Rainbow Card, which was associated for many years with Martina Navratilova, has allowed the financial institution to channel a portion of its return to a number of high-profile GLBT causes and attract thousands of gay cardholders at the same time.

Pride celebrations today are often popular citywide events held during summer and fall that mix activism and celebration with consumerism. National brands, as well as local retailers and service providers, increasingly underwrite these popular events in addition to GLBT film festivals, sporting events, and entertainment that encourage them to put their brand in programs, appear on stage, accept awards, or distribute product samples and discount coupons to a large concentration of GLBT attendees.

Airlines also target incentives for gay group travel with nonprofit partners, and may offer in-kind benefits to organizations as raffle and drawing prizes to assist groups in raising funds. In the past few years, Rosie and Kelli O'Donnell have partnered with Gregg Kaminsky to launch a unique cruise enterprise that offers same-sex partners and their children seaborne vacations with hundreds of similar families. Through this commercial enterprise, R Family Vacations, they partner with corporate brands to highlight causes that are important to these families, such as COLAGE (Children of Lesbians and Gays Everywhere), PFLAG (Parents, Families and Friends of Lesbians and Gays), and the Human Rights Campaign.

FIGURE 8.1 R Family Vacations ad

Source: R Family Vacations. Used with permission.

A reasonable mix of cause and commerce is often as natural as breathing in and out as long as the brand association is respectful, mutually beneficial, and never pandering or exploitative.

STEP 7: MEASURE AND LEARN

For any campaign, there must be ways to measure and track performance. Marketers must try to answer these questions: Was the strategy effective? Has it changed perceptions? Did it add value or quantifiable market share? Has consideration grown for the brand among GLBT households?

Baseline indexes, tracking techniques, and outcome measures are all within our grasp through the conventional survey techniques we use today. They enable us to identify likely GLBT consumers and to index vis-à-vis nongay households. Will they outpace others in their willingness and eagerness to consider and purchase?

More often, major marketers favor the creation of highly targeted pilot programs that roll out messaging and deliverables in one or more geographic markets or market channels. Through an integrated pilot, such as one we conducted for a major automotive brand a few years ago, we designed a creative turnkey campaign that offered purchase incentives, targeted online and print advertising, and participation at nonprofit events to associate with a popular cause in the target market. We learned more through this phase about what truly motivates buyers and grows market share for the brand, and paced the campaign against similar projects targeting other nongay consumers to learn that this approach can and does outperform its peers.

In circumstances when originally conceived elements do not quite seem to work, or the selling proposition or messaging is found to be weak or underperforms, it is much simpler to fine-tune the approach on the fly and to retest the strategy through the pilot and before it is a full-blown effort. Then, the winning pilot strategy can be expanded into a national campaign.

While integrated marketing mixes often provide strong potential, certain media channels make measurement simpler. This is especially true of online strategies that have the capacity to translate impression into sales very swiftly, if executed elegantly. Online metrics, as in all markets, capture the impact, impressions, sustainability, and, most important, sales of a product.

Other measures, however, have worked well too, such as:

- Incentive awards and programs that offer customer bonuses for referring friends and family or buying extra goods or services
- Incentive promotions that deliver nonprofit contributions in exchange for sales
- Affinity programs that offer rewards with membership or participation
- Registration programs that encourage sign-ups in order to receive future offers, information, and product upgrades
- Measurement of impressions, visibility, and receptivity to news articles and product mentions in gay media channels

CHAPTER 9

Out for a Test Drive

As we all know, America's long, long love affair with automobiles goes back more than a century. For decades, millions of our families have invested billions of dollars to own and enjoy the latest triumph on four wheels. Is it any wonder that automakers have so much at stake to win our love and sell their brands? All of us are susceptible to their charms and love to be wooed, right?

What about the GLBT community? It's no surprise that lesbians and gay men share this affinity, and are playing a much more visible role in the marketing strategies of major auto brands. With intense global competition too, there are no customers to be left behind any longer.

Several years ago, the inspiration hit Subaru very hard, as its marketers recognized the appeal of its products to sporty, physically active, and independent women. Subaru was early to the niche marketing table, identifying key lifestyle segments that were already loyal to the brand—outdoor enthusiasts, professionals, and independent thinkers, to name a few. Research conducted in Northampton, Massachusetts, indicated that this community with proportionally higher numbers of lesbian couples was particularly brand loyal to Subaru. Senior management felt it was simply smart marketing to speak to a niche that already existed and that was pretty revolutionary, too.

Subaru executive Tim Bennett and others at the company believed strongly that this connection was real and reachable, if they

FIGURE 9.1 Subaru Ads

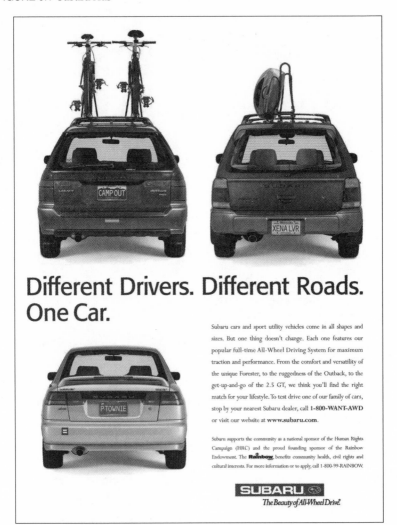

Source: Subaru. Used with permission.

targeted GLBT consumers in a sensitive, creative, and respectful way. Fortunately, Subaru had a seasoned and gifted partner in John Nash and his advertising team at New York–based Moon City Productions. They transformed Subaru's hunch and observations into a series of creative advertising campaigns—in print,

FIGURE 9.1 Subaru Ads *(Continued)*

It's Not a Choice.
It's the Way We're Built.

Subaru All-Wheel Driving System.
In every car we make.

Maximum traction, agility and safety. Experience the performance of the Subaru All-Wheel Driving System in the versatility of the Outback, the ruggedness of the Forester and the get-up-and-go of the Legacy GT Limited. To test drive one of our family of cars, stop by your nearest Subaru dealer, call **1-800-WANT-AWD** or visit our Website at **www.subaru.com**.

Subaru supports the community as the proud founding sponsor of the Rainbow Endowment. The **Rainbow**, benefits health, civil rights and cultural interests. For more information or to apply, call 1-800-99-RAINBOW.

SUBARU
The Beauty of All-Wheel Drive.

online, and even on television—relying on the popular sports legend Martina Navratilova as Subaru's celebrity spokesperson.

To be clear, Navratilova was signed as part of Subaru's outreach to all kinds of active women. Her status as an openly gay tennis player did not concern management; her involvement allowed them to speak in an intelligent and respectful way to Subaru's lesbian customers. The television spots did not scream "lesbian behind the wheel," however; that was not the intention, nor did it ever make a difference. Instead, Navratilova and the early Subaru campaigns generally personified the kinds of Subaru drivers they were seeking, especially strong women with fierce independence, flair, and vitality.

Yet, if Subaru seemed to be early in the pack, it was never really alone. Many leading automotive brands sniffed the clear opportunities, felt the competitive urge, and developed their own campaigns to attract gay car buyers. Even tire brands followed suit, with a multiyear effort launched by Bridgestone that frequently portrayed same-sex couples eager to "accessorize" with its products.

Given the growing market attention and the frequent rediscovery of gay consumers by automotive brands, many questions immediately came to our minds too. For example, what makes a gay consumer choose one car over another? For that matter, what considerations are made by all drivers in deciding what automobile to buy or lease?

Is the choice primarily about body style or the latest trends? Perhaps gas mileage, reliability, safety, or total horsepower are factors that make a real difference. Do different brands speak to consumers in different ways? Well, sure they do, but are these distinctions meaningful to gay drivers in ways that don't mean precisely the same to nongay car buyers?

In 2002, we considered all of these questions, and more. We were excited to put our specialized knowledge and research skills to the test for Volvo Cars of North America in fundamental ways that had never been fully explored before. We were selected that year from a target list of 14 marketing agencies nationwide to help understand the motivations, preferences, likes, and dislikes of gay car owners and buyers.

We simply assumed, as we often do, that what influences a gay car buyer and a nongay one often may be the same kinds of thoughts and opinions. Gay buyers frequently read the same sort of media, talk with their families and friends, remember the familiar dealerships and the kinds of cars their parents most often chose to drive, and like everyone else, consider their wallets perhaps most of all.

In short, what gays think about before they get behind the wheel may often mirror what any future car owner imagines. Similar desires, constraints, impressions, and values based on lifestyles and family needs often go into this fundamental decision.

However, we wondered also what sets gays apart from other consumers, if anything. Gays and lesbians bring to their choices a range of different life stages and some unique mindsets too.

While gays consume much of the same media, they also have specialized newspapers, magazines, and online destinations tailored to their community. Consider also that they frequently have fewer children or none at all, so they might consider the need for far fewer child seats and, instead, desire ample space for dogs, bikes, or beach gear. Even so, the parenting trend is accelerating among same-sex couples, and we are seeing changes in the way some consumers think, particularly lesbian couples who are more apt to raise a child.

What about foreign imports? We wanted to determine, for example, whether gay households find foreign labels more or less appealing. Given the popularity of new technologies like GPS directional capabilities, Bluetooth-enabled wireless phone accessories, and increasingly popular hybrid fuel-efficient engines, we wanted to index whether gay automotive consumers had more or less preference for these upgrades compared to their heterosexual counterparts. Significantly, we also wanted to obtain a true test of brand loyalty. What brands might signal the strongest resonance for gay households specifically?

THE RESEARCH MEETS THE ROAD

In order to better understand the gay, lesbian, bisexual, and transgender consumer segment, therefore, we were commissioned to partner once more with Harris Interactive to conduct an in-depth and unparalleled study to better understand this unique market segment. Volvo was especially intrigued because it understood these basic attributes about gay households:

- The consumer segment's size, estimated to be 13 to 16 million
- The segment's higher discretionary income due to the lower proportionate incidence of children in the household
- The presumed brand loyalty of the segment, especially when GLBT-tailored advertising and marketing tactics are employed

Our research strategy, therefore, sought to identify similarities and differences between GLBT and general population consumer groups relative to automotive behaviors and preferences.

At that time, Harris Interactive's specialty panel had recruited nearly 20,000 gay, lesbian, bisexual, and transgender individual adults across America. Today, we're happy to know that the GLBT specialty panel will soon approach nearly 50,000 self-identified GLBT individuals—the largest online and projectable research panel of its kind that exists anywhere in the world today.

That fall, we then identified and queried 1,000 GLBT consumers along with 1,000 comparable heterosexual consumers about their attitudes, impressions, and consumer behavior related to vehicles. All individuals were qualified adults over the age of 18 and each one held a valid driver's license. More important, all respondents had expressed their intention to buy or lease a car within the next two years. In short, they were qualified automotive consumers.

The in-depth research focused on understanding the gay and lesbian market compared to the general population, including auto buying behavior and use, lifestyle, media consumption, and psychographics. It also would enable us to develop a deeper understanding of the equity of the Volvo brand contrasted with other competitive brand sets among the GLBT and general consumer markets.

Further research explored qualitative findings through an online bulletin board, such as understanding the overall perceptions the Volvo brand and competitors evoked among GLBT consumers, understanding sensitive questions surrounding actual dealership experiences, and assessing GLBT-specific advertising. The effort identified relevant insights that helped inform and were inputs into the development of an effective marketing and advertising campaign for GLBT consumers. We needed not only to understand what gay car buyers were looking for in a product, but also how to talk about it persuasively in a campaign.

An online bulletin board is almost exactly as it sounds. This method is moderated by an unseen online facilitator, and enabled us to present questions, images, and ideas to a select group of qualified individuals across the country. As a "virtual" bulletin board, however, this approach often is a far more convenient use of everyone's time, and enables the busiest of individuals to take the time whenever they can to check out the questions and ideas and respond by posting their reactions and answers. It was an ideal method for our purposes, and allowed several impressions to bubble up from the respondents that guided our knowledge even more.

GUIDING INSIGHTS

The Harris Interactive research confirmed a number of assumptions and validated several key insights about GLBT audiences and their thoughts about cars. Based on this extensive data set, we saw that:

- Among the most important features ranked by GLBT consumers were dependability/reliability, good value, and safety.
- Vehicle environmental friendliness is significantly more important to GLBT consumers than to their heterosexual counterparts.

- GLBT consumers tend to favor imports more than the general population.
- Gay men prefer premium cars more than the general population.
- Lesbians preferred SUVs more than the general population.
- Style mattered more to GLBT consumers than the general population.

As the research dug even deeper, it became apparent that GLBT consumers already had very positive perceptions of the Volvo brand in a number of the areas identified as being important to them, most notably safety, reliability, and value.

With the findings in hand, Volvo then commissioned us to create and launch a smart and innovative marketing and advertising campaign for the GLBT market. We decided then to add an advertising partner to our team for this project, Prime Access, and we turned to agency founder and president Howard Buford and his colleagues to help respond to the creative brief we developed.

"STARTING A FAMILY" CAMPAIGN

Before connecting with one theme, message, and concept, we chose also to test out a few options strategically. The Harris Interactive team partnered with us again to conduct quantitative research to understand reactions to a variety of GLBT ad messages and to more crisply define the creative strategy and develop brand messages that would best resonate with GLBT consumers.

Our advertising team used the results of this research to develop the final ad. We believed strongly, given the findings in our studies, that the GLBT-targeted concept ads should speak directly to GLBT consumers about Volvo's diverse family of vehicles, increase consideration and appreciation for the brand, communicate that GLBT families and Volvo's family of vehicles are diverse and come in all shapes and sizes, and that Volvo is not the stodgy or conventional automotive brand it may sometimes be thought to be.

The more we thought about it, we recognized Volvo already had a very powerful connection with American families, and imagined a strategy that connected also with GLBT families sensitively and intelligently. No other automotive brand had attempted such creative outreach, and we instinctively believed it was a natural path for Volvo that echoed its mainstream appeal as well.

Among several possible creative concepts, we finally selected the "Starting a Family" message because we quickly found that it truly held superior connection with GLBT audiences while communicating the core brand values of safety, quality, understanding today's families, and meeting the needs of Volvo's diverse customers. We also liked the appeal to both men and women, which is sometimes rare in gay marketing campaigns that frequently emphasize or exclusively depict gay male consumers.

"Starting a Family" enabled us to echo a theme that is authentic to the Volvo brand, while resonating with many lesbian and gay adults. The tag literally said, "Whether you're starting a family or creating one as you go." Our point was simple, and a specific way to reflect the realities for many same-sex couples that overcome obstacles to forming their own families. Some are able to parent through advanced medical means, by adopting, or simply by raising children from an earlier marriage. For some gays and lesbians who feel estranged from their birth families at times, we often speak of our "chosen family" among our closest friends. For gays and lesbians, the word *family* itself can take on very large significance, with all of its emotional impact.

The full-color ad execution presented a range of attractive, multiracial families, couples, and individuals in several life stages, as well as very appealing images of Volvo automobiles, in an unforgettable, warm, and appealing mosaic.

In May 2003, we proposed and engineered an integrated campaign around "Starting a Family" that included the ad's presence in national GLBT publications for the next two years. The print campaign was accompanied by an integrated online initiative called "Volvo Family Portraits" on select GLBT Web sites in

FIGURE 9.2 Volvo ad "Starting a Family"

Source: Volvo. Used with permission.

the fall of 2003. With the online component, Volvo customers were invited to tell their own family story, and to describe their feelings about raising kids, forming a household, and simply what made their family lives both ordinary and special. The volunteered essays were extraordinary, honest, funny, moving, and sincere, and helped motivate others to understand the meaning of family and fully appreciate the Volvo brand's commitment to them.

As part of the effort, Volvo also generated a project with the Human Rights Campaign (HRC), the largest gay and lesbian rights organization in the United States, which promoted a generous giveback/purchase offer in conjunction with HRC members. This project further demonstrated Volvo's commitment to the market, which research showed to be a key factor to influence GLBT consumer preference and sustain loyalty from its customers.

We then asked Harris Interactive to go back into the field and ask how many people remembered seeing the ad campaign, and if the consumer was more likely to include Volvo in their consideration set when looking at new vehicles. The findings showed that those GLBT consumers who recognized any element of the campaign were more likely to see Volvo as safe, technically advanced, and a brand that understands the different needs of all of today's families.

The specialized purchase promotion through the Human Rights Campaign also signaled a rising reputation for Volvo among all gay households, who appreciated the respect and attention shown to them by choosing Volvo for purchase or lease in increasing numbers. This was exactly what we had hoped for, in addition to achieving a lasting impression in the market. But the good news for Volvo did not end there.

BREAKING NEW GROUND

After its first successful year, the "Starting a Family" campaign began to make even more waves. In April 2004, Volvo Cars of North America was named a finalist for the esteemed David Ogilvy

FIGURE 9.3 Volvo ad that followed "Starting a Family" entitled "All These Years"

Source: Volvo. Used with permission.

Award for its innovative use of research in advertising by the Advertising Research Foundation (ARF)—the first time in history an Ogilvy honor has been presented to a gay-themed campaign.

We were thrilled to join with our friends at Volvo, as well as Prime Access, to share this unprecedented moment. Presented to advertisers and their partner agencies, the ARF's David Ogilvy Award seeks to showcase successful, innovative, research-driven ad campaigns. From insight to execution to measurement, "Starting a Family" was a solid team effort for a very proud automotive company. To make us all even prouder, in November 2004, the campaign won the Association of National Advertisers (ANA) Multicultural Excellence Award for the best gay and lesbian campaign.

Given this promising debut and track record, we then agreed with our colleagues at Harris Interactive to sustain our growing knowledge and understanding of GLBT auto buyers. We felt then, and even more strongly today, that consumer research propels any company's progress and provides the base for all effective marketing strategies. Therefore, in 2005, we launched the Auto GLB Study, a syndicated study of gay and nongay automotive consumers to analyze brand appeal, features, preferences, tastes, and media consumption patterns, and each year we will plan to repeat, update, and improve this study to meet the needs of many automotive companies and marketers.

CHAPTER 10

Understanding and Managing Backlash

Winning and retaining customers, creating successful marketing initiatives, and helping a company's bottom line are clear rewards for any strategist. Achieving this while also opening up new channels for GLBT consumers has always been important to us.

With every success over the past decade, however, there also occasionally has been some form of discomfort, ignorance, or cultural backlash against companies that choose to advertise or market to gays and lesbians. This also is true of fair-minded companies that adopt internal workplace policies treating their gay employees equally with others.

Gay issues may seem controversial and certainly are unfamiliar to some. When a new gay-friendly policy is disclosed or an advertisement appears there may be questions, complaints, or e-mails, telephone calls, and letters. These consequences so often may be predictable, and reflect evidence of alienation and lack of familiarity with or even troubling hostility toward gays and lesbians. Some of these forms of backlash are based on sincere religious beliefs, upbringing, and outdated family norms. Much of this discomfort, however, is also based on lack of knowledge and familiarity.

The good news is that every year respected polls show convincingly that more Americans recognize they have gay family members, co-workers, neighbors, and friends. The more familiar Americans are with gays, lesbians, bisexuals, and transgender peo-

ple, surveys also show significantly higher trends toward acknowledgement and acceptance, and, consequently, fewer fears and much
less ignorance about gays. Dramatic evidence of acceptance especially may be found among younger people from all walks of
life, as well as among women and more highly educated people.

For example, in the summer of 2005, according to a survey au-
thorized by the Pew Trust, a majority of Americans for the first time
said they favored either legal same-sex marriage or civil unions
for gay couples. This notable shift represents a significant move
forward on a hot button issue in a relatively short time frame.

While attitudes show progress, when complaints or some
forms of spontaneous backlash emerge, it is reassuring to understand it is nearly always short-lived too. Most companies appear
to evidence a brief period—perhaps a few days or a few weeks—
when they feel called to respond to customers and to critical inquiries. It is rare for these episodes to persist. Almost all individuals find that expressing their feelings and having them heard
and respectfully acknowledged can go a long way.

Businesses have learned from experience to respond in a low-
key, businesslike fashion to these forms of discomfort and to treat
them with the same businesslike respect they give all others.
However, only in the rarest circumstances is there evidence of a
management decision to retreat entirely, abandon a marketing
strategy, or rescind its gay-inclusive policies based on hostile or
critical feedback. Turning back the clock and shifting course are
also seen by the market as unprincipled and waffling. These ambiguous signals raise eyebrows and questions from the media,
customers, and shareholders alike.

Time and again companies have learned to understand, acknowledge, and manage these predictable episodes. They generally
avoid inflaming the circumstances by overreacting, stonewalling,
generating unwanted press coverage, or appearing to pick a brawl.
All of those heavy-handed practices are unhelpful at best and dangerous at worst.

Corporate leaders sincerely believe they must respond authen-
tically to the needs of a diverse, growing, and highly segmented

market, and that including gays and lesbians within their policies and practices is smart business. They do so to remain competitive, be consistent with their policies, and recognize all of their employees, customers, shareholders, and vendors.

WHAT ABOUT THE THREAT OF BOYCOTTS?

There was a time when polite conversation in the American workplace largely steered clear of politics or religion. From the boardroom to the water cooler, factory floor to showroom, most of us understood or tacitly agreed that polite conversation exited when religious beliefs and political opinions entered. However, our political and corporate cultures have changed, and we have witnessed many of those shifts over the last decade in our work.

Now businessmen and businesswomen frequently are forced to grapple with provocative issues they'd just as soon avoid. Companies feel the strain of being caught in the crossfire by making business calculations and market choices on a host of sensitive questions such as these:

- Should employee health care coverage include family planning, birth control, and abortion services?
- Can companies safely sponsor television spots on programs with controversial or edgy content?
- What are obligations of Hollywood and the music industry for responsibly presenting explicit sexuality and defiant subject matter?
- Should companies assist with adoptions for employees who are single, partnered, or married?

THE MOST SENSITIVE ISSUES TODAY

With changing attitudes and contemporary cultural shifts, it is not difficult for any company to find itself trying to grapple with social issues that affect its market, its workforce, its customers, and, above all, its reputation. Yet of all social issues facing business, perhaps few are more sensitive or more likely to grab public attention than the acceptance, inclusion, and recognition of gay and lesbian employees, customers, and shareholders.

As GLBT people become more visible and a growing force in the economy, how will business respond? How should companies respond? For instance, should management include the domestic partners of gay employees for the same package of health benefits given to married heterosexual couples? How can a company successfully market to lesbian and gay households without inspiring discomfort at best or distracting and vociferous protest at worst?

We have dedicated our practice to helping corporations and decision makers successfully respond to these questions, and to design effective communications strategies for coping with backlash risk while building smart market choices that include gay customers and gay employees. Our real-world experiences must remain confidential; however, the lessons and guidelines we've developed are invaluable and we wish to share them with everyone.

Several years ago, recall that one of America's most conservative religious denominations, the leaders of the Southern Baptist Convention, launched a highly publicized boycott against the Walt Disney Company, one of the world's best-known entertainment corporations.

Disney's social critics assaulted the company with a laundry list of complaints, including: commercializing smut and violence in film and television; recognizing homosexuality in Disney-owned programming like *Ellen,* starring openly lesbian Ellen DeGeneres; and appearing to sanction Gay Days at Disney theme parks. Like most corporations, of course, Disney was focused on conducting its business, developing profitable entertainment properties, and welcoming all visitors without discrimination.

Worse, in the eyes of the Southern Baptists, the Disney Company—along with virtually all of its film industry peers and a majority of Fortune 500 companies today—began to offer health benefits for the same-gender partners of Disney employees, as they do for married couples. For true believers, this may have been the last straw. To the extreme right, this step mirrored the benefits of marriage for same-sex couples, which they adamantly oppose.

Disney was neither the first nor would it be the last company to feel the heat. Many of America's favorite brands and most visible corporate leaders have felt the sting from radical right-wing interest groups. These attacks reflect some of America's discomfort and unfamiliarity with the evolutionary changes taking place in society and are about a cultural divide that is more manipulated than real.

Conservative firebrands and right-wing fundraisers routinely challenge corporate policies that stray from what they mislabel "traditional family values," especially with regard to gay and lesbian employees. In the past decade alone, corporate targets have included a who's who in American business life, including American Express, IBM, AT&T, Bank of America, Wells Fargo, Walgreens, Levi Strauss, Kraft, Procter & Gamble, American Airlines, Microsoft, Ford Motor Company, and IKEA, as well as countless others. It is safe to predict that virtually no company is invulnerable to being criticized for addressing issues of concern to gays and lesbians.

NEW BATTLEGROUND ON SAME-SEX MARRIAGE

With incremental progress underway in the legal recognition of same-sex relationships—from civil unions in Vermont in 2000 and Connecticut in 2005 to equal marriage rights in Massachusetts in 2004 and domestic partner registries in several states—it is no wonder that the debate about same-sex couples has become so politically charged. Like the American people, companies also are highly sensitive to these sea changes.

The U.S. elections held in 2004 brought these debates home for everyone. In a historic year when same-sex marriage became legal in Massachusetts, the issue to restrict or ban the recognition of marriage between gay couples, not surprisingly, found its way onto 11 ballot measures. In fact, voters in Arkansas, Georgia, Kentucky, Michigan, Mississippi, Montana, Ohio, Oklahoma, Oregon, North Dakota, and Utah passed measures limiting or banning the legal recognition of same-sex relationships.

But that is not the whole story by a long shot, or a complete picture about American attitudes toward gays and lesbians and their same-sex relationships. It is important to understand these attitudes as clearly as possible and to put them into perspective. Does public support for antimarriage measures signify that Americans are increasingly hostile toward gays and lesbians, or that they are less accepting than they have been in the past? Is backlash likely to be a more serious consequence in our culture and for corporations? We firmly believe the actual evidence says otherwise.

What Happened in 2004?

The marriage ballot measures were not the only word on gay issues and political candidates, however. In 2004, American voters also:

- Voted in many races to elect and reelect openly gay candidates throughout the nation
- Elected or reelected all six GLBT candidates running for legislative offices in California
- Elected open lesbians to North Carolina's state senate, to the Idaho state house, and to the Missouri state house
- Elected the first-ever openly lesbian Latina as sheriff in Dallas County, Texas
- Reelected every Massachusetts lawmaker on the ballot, Democrat and Republican, gay and straight, who supported gay rights
- Enacted a ballot measure in Cincinnati *to repeal* a law that prevents the city from passing legislation to protect gays and lesbians from discrimination (this favorable result occurred in a state that also adopted a state constitutional ban on same-sex marriage)

AMERICAN PUBLIC OPINION TRENDS
ARE MORE FAVORABLE TODAY

Over the past few years, numerous national and state surveys confirm that a majority of Americans are still troubled by legal marriage for same-sex couples. It is not really surprising, therefore, that ballot measures against legal marriage for gays and lesbians have succeeded.

When probed, however, we also discover that many Americans do not distinguish clearly between the matrimonial sacraments of marriage bestowed by churches, temples, or mosques and the civil sanction of marriage conferred by state law. Whether through tradition or faith, many Americans evidently do not wish to confuse their long-held definitions of marriage by endorsing equal married status for gay couples—even if churches and their faith are separate considerations.

But that is not all Americans believe. In many of the very same surveys, including the Pew findings cited above, a majority of Americans specifically favor establishing some forms of advanced legal protections for gay and lesbian couples. This was also confirmed in the same exit polls taken in 2004:

> When asked specifically in the 2004 exit polls, one-quarter or 25 percent of voters favored legal marriage for same-sex couples, while 37 percent opposed any form of legal recognition.
>
> Most important, over a third of all voters asked—35 percent— stated they favor some form of legal relationship such as a civil union, yet not labeled or defined specifically as a marriage. Therefore, 60 percent, or six out of ten adults, support some form of legal recognition for gay couples.

Under normal circumstances in American life, a 60 percent to 37 percent margin would be considered very decisive. This emerging consensus also is validated by survey research conducted in 2003 and 2004 by Witeck-Combs Communications and Harris Interactive when we queried over 2,000 American adults about eligibility for workplace benefits, such as health and life insurance coverage, adoption assistance, and survivorship benefits. Employment benefits often mirror the same privileges and rights conferred by marital status, and are a valid way to examine acceptance of gays and lesbians.

Specifically, when heterosexuals were asked whether certain benefits of employment now available to married spouses should be equally available to same-sex partners, in almost every instance, nearly two-thirds of heterosexuals agree that equal treatment ought to be given to employees with same-sex partners. They see this as fundamentally fair and reasonable.

The specific benefits included the taxability of health insurance benefits, adoption assistance, bereavement leave, relocation assistance for partners, family and medical leave emergencies, and COBRA health coverage. In fact, in each instance, support grew by at least 4 percent to 5 percent between 2003 and 2004, even after same-sex marriage became a reality in Massachusetts.

Same-sex marriage itself is likely to remain a sensitive, sometimes politically charged question; however, Americans not only are more aware of gays and lesbians in society but also increasingly fair-minded in terms of acceptance and treatment of their intimate relationships. Factors of age, education, and gender also play roles in terms of acceptance. More welcoming attitudes are consistently associated with younger people, women, and people with higher education. All of these trends are important to underscore for American business too.

The better news is that overall understanding and acceptance continues to grow. Increasing numbers of Americans, according to research, also believe homosexuality is an innate and unchangeable characteristic and that gays and lesbians cannot be and ought not be changed. With those shifts in opinion and understanding, it is far more likely that acceptance can and will follow too.

MARKET TRENDS FOLLOW PUBLIC OPINION TOO

At the end of 2003, as significant indicators, over 40 percent of Fortune 500 companies and 68 percent of the Fortune 50 offered equal benefits for same-sex couples. Over 7,000 employers across the U.S. now provide health insurance coverage to an employee's same-sex domestic partner, a trend that is currently growing at the rate of 18 percent more companies each year.

In 2005, in fact, 101 corporations earned the highest marks from the Human Rights Campaign and its Corporate Equality Index for their fair-minded employment and workplace policies—treating their employees with committed same-sex partners equal in virtually all instances to their married employees.

The Human Rights Campaign Foundation's Corporate Equality Index is a simple and effective tool to rate large American businesses on how they are treating gay, lesbian, bisexual, and transgender employees, consumers, and investors.

Companies were rated on a scale of 0 percent to 100 percent on seven criteria, based on whether they:

- Have a written nondiscrimination policy covering sexual orientation in their employee handbook or manual
- Have a written nondiscrimination policy covering gender identity and/or expression in their employee handbook or manual
- Offer health insurance coverage to employees' same-sex domestic partners
- Officially recognize and support a gay, lesbian, bisexual, and transgender employee resource group; or would support employees forming a GLBT employee resource group, if some expressed interest, by providing space and other resources; or have a company-wide diversity council or working group whose mission specifically includes GLBT diversity
- Offer diversity training that includes sexual orientation and/or gender identity and expression in the workplace

- Engage in respectful and appropriate marketing to the gay, lesbian, bisexual, and transgender community and/or provide support through their corporate foundation or otherwise to GLBT or HIV/AIDS-related organizations or events
- Engage in corporate action that would undermine the goal of equal rights for gay, lesbian, bisexual, and transgender people

The trend toward recognition and equal treatment of gay couples in corporate America is based frequently on many corporations' stated desire to treat all employees and their families fairly and equally, as well as competitive pressures to recruit and retain the best qualified workers including GLBT people.

Interestingly, in 2004, two states and 66 cities and counties, according to the Human Rights Campaign, also provide domestic partner registries—another independent means to recognize same-sex couples. In 2007, the state of California will also join a trend started by San Francisco, Los Angeles, Minneapolis, Seattle, and New York to require companies that do business with local or state government to offer benefits to gay couples that are equal to those currently available to heterosexual, married couples.

Equal treatment and basic fairness toward gays and lesbians remain clear trends in public policy decisions and employment practices from coast to coast. They frequently motivate employers and local communities to establish innovative approaches to respect gay couples and to achieve a level of parity under the law and contemporary custom.

WHAT IS BACKLASH?

Most recognize backlash when they see it, and, of course, public anxiety about a company can take many forms.

The instigated arsenal may take shape through paid advertising, direct mail fundraising appeals, online and Web site activism, postcard campaigns, unflattering and unwanted media stories, radio evangelism, occasional picket lines, and even undisguised threats on Capitol Hill. The point is to drive a wedge between consumers and the company, and to invoke public shame and market retribution against alleged corporate offenders.

For CEOs and corporate communicators, these dramas can be real enough even if the confrontations are staged. Within the business community, we have seen how controversy can be a heartstopper over the bottom line and a perceived threat to a company's reputation and ability to conduct its business.

This climate, taken to an extreme, begs important questions for corporate decision makers:

- Does archconservative backlash really stir up lasting resentment, lost sales, or erosion of shareholder value?
- What are the lessons for experienced communicators, and how are culture conflicts different from other kinds of protests or consumer boycotts in years past?
- How does business responsibly balance these issues and address these challenges when the critics' flames torch their products and their good name?

The corporate strategist today acknowledges that familiar rules of engagement may not apply any longer. This is especially true when commerce and culture mix and collide. Therefore, here are the new rules that companies are learning and putting into practice. Above all, successful companies are focused on their business mission and sustaining their corporate identity and values.

Rule 1: Never Confuse Political Dogma with Faith

As a first step, it's important to acknowledge that, for some individuals, discomfort as well as ignorance about gay people is real. Some Americans are confused, anxious, and even angry about gays and lesbians, and do not wish to associate with them or recognize their place in society. Some of these attitudes are generational and signaled by religious and parental upbringing; many people outgrow these feelings or put them into context and acceptance. Others do not.

It is wrong, however, to minimize or marginalize what people firmly believe, and companies are never in the business to change people's personal convictions or challenge their sincerely held religious values. Instead, a company must find ways to bridge differences, both internal and external, in order to conduct its business. Using religion or faith as a weapon, however, is distracting, dangerous, and inappropriate in the world of commerce.

While sincere religious beliefs are acceptable, experience shows that antigay groups in America generally reflect political dogma, not genuine spirituality. The architects of anticorporate backlash strategies have never spoken for all people of faith, or for all churches.

The radical conservative agenda in the United States today is led by well-organized and well-funded interest groups. Though cloaked frequently in sanctimony, their tools are membership organizing, communications, marketing and publicity, and fundraising appeals that pander almost entirely to fear and loathing. These strategies are designed to set the cultural agenda for legislation, judicial appointments, ballot measures, and the election of like-minded candidates for public office.

Dogmatic and extreme interest groups unfairly yet shrewdly demonize gays and lesbians while attempting to intimidate corporate America—assuming corporations consent to be intimidated. Smart corporations never offer their consent.

Rule 2: Faith Does Deserve Respect, but Diversity More So

America's most successful and forward-thinking companies understand inclusiveness and apply diversity principles intelligently. They reflect all of their employees and their customers, and use this knowledge of the changing market and workforce. Not all families look alike any longer. By mirroring society's change, business executives acknowledge differences and offer equal treatment as an ethical business objective, and not as agents pushing social change.

That's why corporations such as IBM, Mobil, Eastman Kodak, Wachovia, Fannie Mae, BankBoston, Citigroup, American Express and many more (not to mention cities like Chicago, New York, and Philadelphia) were determined to provide domestic partner benefits for same-sex couples. They see this as a competitive measure. Recruiting and retaining all qualified professionals as a marketplace imperative also allows them to better respond to a valuable consumer niche. And as an equity principle, it is aimed to treat all their employees fairly and equally.

Within exceptional diversity programs, for example, not only do devoutly Christian employees and gay and lesbian employees work side by side, but they do so with Muslims, Jews, Hispanics, Asian-Americans, African-Americans, and people with disabilities, among others. It is exasperating at times, when corporate managers polarize the concept of diversity by suggesting that gays and lesbians are a distinct group from people of faith. It ought to be very clear that many GLBT people also find religion and spirituality important in their personal lives, and often attend their denomination's worship services too or perhaps the churches they were raised in as children.

Mainstream religious denominations, moreover, are often invested in the American civil rights tradition. Here companies find respect and opportunity and not backlash or boycotts. Smart companies not only value and respect all employees and consumers, but they acknowledge and reinforce legitimate ties among the religious faithful.

The mainstream faiths and traditions among Roman Catholics, Protestants, Jews, Muslims, and others have a history of appropriate engagement with the broader civil rights movement. Religious groups such as the Interfaith Alliance and the long-respected National Leadership Conference on Civil Rights, for example, bring most of these denominations together to work on civil rights issues. They start by welcoming and respecting differences and not by exacerbating and polarizing them. Religious expression, therefore, does not foster belligerence; nor does it generally bless boycotts against companies.

Rule 3: Stay True to Your Business Mission and Your Message

Companies can successfully withstand outside pressures without sacrificing their core beliefs, employee morale, customer trust, or market share.

Surely customers deserve to be heard and receive respectful responses, even angry and disgruntled customers. However, businesses also deserve to sell their products and services in the marketplace and to determine their own employment and marketing policies.

Let's reflect again about the Walt Disney Company and the consequences of the often-publicized, seven-year Southern Baptist boycott. As the business media widely reported, during the years of the "official" boycott, the Disney theme parks frequently posted record attendance and profits among most of its business divisions, including its films, books, publications, and television programs. The Disney Company channeled its response primarily in two directions: first, by remaining consistent in its welcoming and inclusive business philosophy; and second, and most important, by doing what it does best—creating products and entertainment options that are broadly popular with most Americans (and most people around the world).

In the past few years, other companies such as Kraft Foods and Procter & Gamble also recognized that their best strategy was little or no direct response to attacks. It is tough to stage a clamorous public debate or to hijack a company to the woodshed if the company refuses to be led there. Most companies understand that their corporate objectives are best served by withstanding unreasonable and unreasoned attacks and by taking principled businesslike stands and sticking to them. Those are modest but powerful actions that influence Wall Street and Main Street.

Research conducted over the years by a number of respected pollsters and by television networks also underscore that most Americans are unaware of boycott threats and that fewer still comply with demands to shun a company for moral reasons. The right to complain and to protest certainly is as American as apple pie; however, actual market behaviors are another matter.

In early 2006, in the wake of several publicized threats against companies from Microsoft and Procter & Gamble to Nike, Ford, Kraft Foods, and Hewlett-Packard, Witeck-Combs Communications and Harris Interactive asked more than 3,000 adult heterosexuals their feelings about such boycotts. Specifically, we wanted to know whether they favor or oppose boycotts against companies that market and advertise to gays and lesbians.

Nearly six out of ten (58 percent) of all Americans said they oppose these threats—with four out of ten (42 percent) saying they strongly oppose boycotts and another quarter (24 percent) of the sample registering no opinion at all. A mere 8 percent said they strongly favor boycotts against gay-friendly marketers. Still, real-world experience also shows that of the scant few who register hostility in the marketplace, fewer of them follow through on their feelings or demonstrate a measurable market impact.

Companies build bankable trust by communicating clearly and consistently, and by being armed with a brief, straightforward statement that reinforces the company's overarching business policies. Companies do not choose to engage in argumentative rebuttal (though they are entitled to clear up all misstatements of fact aimed at them) or combative wordplay.

A confident, measured, and brief response is intended for the broader audience and the marketplace, but not as a weapon to reply. It is impossible to persuade all or to get every critic to agree, but a firm, businesslike stand will impress most by its integrity and consistency.

Many Americans often perceive public attacks as bullying, shrill, unbalanced, and very often misleading if not entirely inaccurate. Fortunately—and in almost every instance—they also tend to be short-lived and leave few lasting traces. Critics and interest groups typically lurch from target to target, seeking their best near-term opportunity to focus on a corporate prey and then to capture headlines, raise dollars, and energize and recruit members.

PRINCIPLE OF FREE MARKET ADVERTISING EXPRESSION

To underscore the market's united voice in standing up for business principles and to oppose antigay backlash, industry leaders from the American Association of Advertising Agencies (AAAA) and the Association of National Advertisers took an unprecedented step in the spring of 2006. The two associations joined with the Commercial Closet Association to endorse the Principle of Free Market Advertising Expression, which simply said in two sentences:

> *In America, all companies have the basic right to determine their own market expression—by advertising and selling to all customers respectfully and inclusively. We oppose all forms of attacks intended to disrupt free commerce based on intolerance and hostility toward any consumer, including gay, lesbian, bisexual, and transgender people.*

Corporate leaders, including the advertising community, draw a logical distinction between old-fashioned conservativism and today's ultramoralism, especially when the latter tries to strangle prudent business decisions and is intended to drive a wedge among consumers and within the marketplace for controversy's sake. As far as most business leaders are concerned, it ought to be a sin to interfere with capitalistic acts between consenting adults.

Appendix A

Resources, Experts, and Allies

We all need friends, allies, and copilots when we enter new, unexplored, or unfamiliar terrain. Fortunately for marketers eager to do their homework and to truly understand the gay, lesbian, bisexual, and transgender community, there are trusted navigators, reliable signposts, and a wealth of emerging resources. There also are diverse numbers of respected organizations, business groups, and academics that have unselfishly contributed to our knowledge as we have shared ours in return.

This appendix will highlight many of the most productive connections, experts, and resources, often available online or by diving headfirst into their published reports, studies, Web sites, projects, and books. We frequently cite our own nonproprietary public opinion surveys conducted over the past six years with our research partner, Harris Interactive. Rather than list all of these reports here, let's keep it simple.

We invite you to come directly to our Web site, *www.witeckcombs .com*, which presents a wide selection of specialized news reports on market and public policy issues. Many of these surveys may also be found through Harris Interactive at *www.harrisinteractive .com*, along with very useful background on the company's methodology. We are not pollsters; however, working alongside our partners at Harris Interactive, we strongly subscribe to the sound principles for public disclosure of research data that are maintained by the National Council on Public Polls *(www.ncpp.org)*.

GETTING DOWN TO BUSINESS

There are no fewer than six nonprofit groups in the GLBT community that focus, in part or in full, on marketplace and workplace issues as their mission. They advance our knowledge of the business community, progressive workplace practices, and workplace organizing, as well as marketing and advertising strategies that assist corporate America. These organizations include:

- **The Workplace Project of the Human Rights Campaign Foundation** (HRC), *www.hrc.org*

  The HRC Workplace Project is widely known for its sound data on corporate human resources policies and workplace practices along with the much-admired annual Corporate Equality Index (CEI) and the new consumer-friendly *Buying for Equality Guide* that offers GLBT households a practical tool to identify gay-friendly companies at which to shop. These tools are available on the HRC Web site with many other essential tools and archives.

  This year, the Human Rights Campaign Foundation applied its knowledge to a new resource entitled "The Best Places to Work," which also relies on this valuable business data. In 2004 and 2005, Wes Combs co-chaired the HRC Business Council, which advises the HRC and the HRC Foundation on leading business practices and is served by member volunteers from a cross-section of leading U.S. corporations.

- **Out & Equal Workplace Advocates,** *www.outandequal.org*

  This San Francisco–based national nonprofit organization with chapters in major U.S. cities offers an invaluable network of corporate professionals who work within their own GLBT employee resource groups to help effect equal policies, opportunities, practices, and benefits at work regardless of sexual orientation or gender identity, expression, or characteristics. Out & Equal holds its annual workplace summit, the largest event of its kind that brings together human resource, marketing, and executive participants whose common goal is to make workplaces equal for all employees. Throughout the year, it also conducts professional programming through its chapters and its national office.

■ **National Gay & Lesbian Chamber of Commerce** (NGLCC), *www.nglcc.org*

Throughout the United States, many cities and communities have fostered networks of GLBT professionals, entrepreneurs, and business owners. Over the years, these networks have evolved to become local chambers of commerce that deliver meaningful business and professional advancement programs for their business owners and professional members.

The National Gay & Lesbian Chamber of Commerce emerged just a few years ago to give a long-awaited national voice to these GLBT business leaders and to build practical bridges for major corporations wishing to partner and associate with them. Among NGLCC programs, perhaps the most prized is its supplier certification initiative that helps corporations identify and procure competitive services from gay-owned entrepreneurs, much as these corporations do with other minority small business associations today.

■ **Commercial Closet Association,** *www.commercialcloset.org*

Founded by journalist Mike Wilke, the Commercial Closet Association is a nonprofit educational association that works within the business world and among advertising agencies to bring about more inclusive and respectful representations of the GLBT community in all forms of advertising and marketing. With its popular Web site, rich with hundreds of creative representations of GLBT characters, themes, and ideas, it is visited often by students, ad agency professionals, media planners, marketers, and journalists to review trends and see firsthand negative and positive portrayals in the marketplace.

Among its most valuable contributions, however, may be the specialized counsel given through its Best Practices for agencies seeking to include GLBT representations in ad campaigns.

■ **Equality Project,** *www.equalityproject.org*

Shareholder activism and investor education also have long been part of the lexicon for gay workplace advocates, and this is the primary mission of the Equality Project, based in New York City. Founded in 1993, this nonprofit group describes itself as a consumer, employee, and investor advocacy coalition working to support and monitor workplace awareness and adoption of the progressive policies expressed in its Equality Principles, which are similar (though not identical) in substance to the HRC's Corporate Equality Index. The work of this group is to advocate for fair and equal corporate practices through the voice of the investor community and large fund holders.

■ **Pride at Work,** *www.prideatwork.org*

While the Equality Project works on the shareholder front, Pride at Work is the gay, lesbian, bisexual, and transgender constituency group of the AFL-CIO. Through this nonprofit, GLBT union representatives are out and organizing within the labor and GLBT movement nationwide.

ACADEMIC AND RESEARCH LEADERS

Our debt to social scientists, demographers, and researchers is very real and often personal. There are a range of leading academics and writers who have advanced the knowledge of the GLBT community and also to add insight about the contributions we make to business, commerce, and entrepreneurialism.

We proudly recommend greater attention be paid to their specialized contributions, studies, and books, such as:

- Dr. Lee. V. Badgett, Dr. Gary Gates, and their chief sponsors, Brad Sears and Bill Rubenstein at the Williams Project, University of California at Los Angeles, *www.law.ucla.edu/ williamsproj/.* The Williams Project, founded in 2001 by a generous philanthropist, is an academic center at UCLA Law School to study sexual orientation law and public policy. By bringing together a dedicated team of expert social scientists, legal minds, and demographers, this think tank is making remarkable waves in advancing knowledge about GLBT lives, families, and households to inform the media, lawmakers, and society. In 2006, the Williams Project also will merge with the independent, East Coast–based think tank, the Institute for Gay & Lesbian Strategic Studies *(www.iglss.org)* conceived and led by Dr. Lee Badgett.

  Badgett's emphasis over several years has been on the economic behaviors and income distribution of gays and lesbians, as well as on significant public policy questions on the cost and implications of equal partner benefits. Her breakthrough book, *Money, Myths and Change: The Economic Lives of Lesbians and Gay Men* (University of Chicago, 2003), helped educate marketers and social scientists and dispelled the myth of affluence some have maintained about the GLBT population. We find this work compelling and valuable for each of us in recognizing gay and lesbian perspectives on financial and family decisions—as well as their professional lives—and issues that affect gay livelihoods, such as workplace discrimination, denial of health care benefits to partners and children, the corporate wooing of gay consumer dollars, and the use of gay economic clout to inspire social and political change.

- The publication of *The Gay and Lesbian Atlas* (Urban Institute, 2004), coauthored by Dr. Gary Gates and Jason Ost, has had a similar transformative educational value. Relying on the very best empirical evidence available anywhere—the Census 2000 household data—Gates and Ost provide the deepest framework yet for gathering evidence of same-sex partnered households throughout the United States. More than an atlas, this social science primer helps clarify the geographic, racial, and gender makeup of America's same-sex coupled population. Imperfect and incomplete as this partner data may be in mapping the entire GLBT community, it remains a powerful head start for all who wish to reach these households and to understand them better.

Advanced scholarship on gay and lesbian public policy and market issues now also may be found at a broad number of academic centers throughout the U.S., and we may single out only a few who particularly stand out for their influence and expertise on gay market, economic, workplace, and media issues, including:

- Dr. Gregory Herek, University of California at Davis, internationally recognized as an authority on sexual prejudice (also called *homophobia*), hate crimes, and AIDS stigma. His Web site, Sexual Orientation: Science, Education, and Policy *(http://psychology.ucdavis.edu/rainbow/index.html)* provides factual information to promote the use of scientific knowledge for education and enlightened public policy related to sexual orientation and HIV/AIDS.

- Dr. Ken Sherrill, professor of political science at Hunter College, City University of New York, is a leading political, media, and cultural theorist on the GLBT community, and often researches the intersection between political awareness, policy, and gay issues such as same-sex marriage.

- Dr. Larry Gross, professor of communication at the University of California's Annenberg School for Communication, is considered one of the founders of the field of gay and lesbian studies, and is well-known for his vitally important work, *Up From Invisibility: Lesbians, Gay Men, and the Media in America* (Columbia University Press, 2002).

Gross is a widely quoted and respected specialist in the areas of media and culture, art and communication, visual communication, and media portrayals of minorities.

- Dr. Katherine Sender, protégé of Professor Larry Gross and currently assistant professor at Penn's Annenberg Center, is herself an accomplished scholar on gay media representations and market research, and the author of the critical book, *Business, Not Politics: The Making of the Gay Market* (Columbia University Press, 2005).
- Dr. Tracy Tuten Ryan, assistant professor of advertising research at Virginia Commonwealth University, has advanced valuable knowledge about gay responses to advertising and other forms of business communication.

In 2002 and again in 2004, we partnered with Packaged Facts, a highly respected team of market research analysts, to produce *The U.S. Gay and Lesbian Market.* This report offers a compendium of the best available market knowledge of GLBT households found anywhere and helps segment harder-to-find segments of the population including youth, seniors, families, and people of color. More details on this biannual study—the next edition is due in the fall of 2006—may be found at *www.marketresearch.com.*

In addition to the comprehensive consumer knowledge found in the *Gay and Lesbian Market Report,* Hyperion Interactive Media now publishes an annual guide on the media channels—online, print, radio, television, events—that serve the GLBT population exclusively. As a primary source for media background, it is proving to be a very reliable tool and may be found for purchase online at *www.himcorp.com.*

To assist marketers and other organizations to connect with GLBT media nationally, since 2002, we also have established an exclusive partnership with U.S. Newswire. U.S. Newswire today is recognized as the leading public interest newswire service in the nation. Among its clients are the White House Press Office, Congressional committees, and public interest groups of all description. We have tapped their unique resources to create the largest, most reliable, targeted distribution of news releases and related materials to the GLBT media through its electronic wire service feed, as well as broadcast fax, e-mail, satellite, and other Internet-based news delivery services. This service may be found online at *www.usnewswire.com/services_lesbian&gay.html*.

To serve advertisers well, we also collaborate frequently with the community's leading media broker, Rivendell Media *(www .rivendellmedia.com)*, which represents a majority of the nation's leading gay and lesbian and HIV/AIDS publications. In addition, in league with Prime Access, a top multicultural advertising agency, Rivendell Media tracks and publishes an annual advertising report segmented by industry sector that measures all advertising in gay print media year over year. *The Gay Press Report* is an indispensable index for media planners, advertisers, and business and trade media interested in evaluating the growth and spread of advertising targeted to gay households.

COMMUNITY LEADERSHIP AND GLBT MEMBERSHIP GROUPS

More than 15 million Americans united by their identity as sexual minorities are richly represented by a broad range of civil rights groups, public interest causes, membership organizations, recreational and sporting groups, and faith-based organizations.

In search of connections, GLBT people often are eager to find trusted ways to assert their common identity, advocate for causes they share, and meet significant others and make friends. More companies every year are eager to develop cause-related partnerships and sponsorships with these community leaders as a way to grow incremental market share, enhance their corporate reputation, and signal their public commitment to diversity, inclusion, and fair treatment.

While it is impossible to list the hundreds of organizations within the broad GLBT community, these national organizations and causes stand out for their visibility in the media and popularity with members and donors. Each has a Web site identified for more details and contact information:

- **The Human Rights Campaign,** *www.hrc.org*

  The Human Rights Campaign is America's largest GLBT civil rights group with over a half-million members and donor-activists. Founded more than 25 years ago, the Human Rights Campaign performs advocacy on a broad range of federal public policy, referenda, and legislative issues. It effectively supports and connects civil rights advocates in every part of the nation and publishes a well-known quarterly magazine called *Equality,* which also allows corporate sponsors and partners to advertise.

- **The National Lesbian & Gay Task Force,** *www.thetask force.org*

  The Task Force was founded in 1973, and therefore is deemed the oldest national gay rights group in the United States. It is focused on building grassroots political strength by training state and local activists and leaders, and strengthening the infrastructure of state and local allies that grow public support for complete equality for GLBT people.

- **Gay & Lesbian Alliance Against Defamation** (GLAAD), *www.glaad.org*

  Best known for its prestigious media awards, GLAAD advocates for accurate, fair, and balanced representations of the GLBT community in all forms of news and entertainment media.

- **Parents, Families and Friends of Lesbians and Gays** (PFLAG), *www.pflag.org*

  PFLAG speaks primarily for the families and friends of gays, lesbians, bisexuals, and transgender people, and may be found most often working within communities to make them safer, more welcoming, and accepting of all.

- **Gay, Lesbian, Straight Education Network** (GLSEN), *www .glsen.org*

America's safe schools movement is aligned closely with GLSEN and helps establish a vital bridge among educators, parents, and students who work hard to make all school settings tolerant and respectful of differences, particularly for GLBT students and adults.

- **Lambda Legal Defense and Education Fund,** *www.lambdalegal.org*

The attorneys and legal advocates who created the Lambda Legal Defense and Education Fund in 1973 recognized the challenges of working within our existing legal system and court structure to defend and advance the civil rights of the GLBT community. Like the ACLU and similar organizations, Lambda works voluntarily today to develop precedent-setting law to provide equal protection, fair treatment, and unbiased recognition of same-sex relationships for all GLBT people.

- **National Youth Advocacy Coalition,** *www.nyac.org*

GLBT youth and supportive youth advocates connect through this remarkable network of teen and twenty-something individuals across the country. Given the unacceptably high rates of teen suicide and substance abuse for GLBT youth, this group is focused on all strategies to support, protect, and nurture these at-risk individuals.

- **National Black Justice Coalition** (NBJC), *www.nbjc.org*

This is the nation's leading national civil rights group primarily for people of color in the GLBT community. NBJC works through education and advocacy to respond and oppose racism and homophobia in all communities.

- **Mautner Project, the National Lesbian Health Organization,** *www.mautnerproject.org*

According to ample research, lesbians are less inclined to seek preventive health care in the face of discrimination and homophobia. Given this challenge, the Mautner Project works to educate lesbians about their health and trains health care providers about their lesbian patients, providing tools and insights on how to achieve better health outcomes for lesbians. It has become the national voice on health care on behalf of lesbians and bisexual women.

- **International Gay and Lesbian Travel Association** (IGLTA), *www.iglta.org*

  The IGLTA is a global industry association of gay and gay-friendly market leaders in the travel, tourism, and hospitality industries. Their purpose is to advance the industry as a whole while advocating on behalf of the GLBT community's needs to safely and enjoyably travel to all destinations.

- **The International Association of Lesbian, Gay, Bisexual and Transgender Pride Coordinators,** also known as Inter-Pride, *www.interpride.org*

  This organization serves as the official network association of all GLBT pride events throughout the United States. Gay pride observances may take many forms but are often known to include parades, marches, rallies, arts and other kinds of festivals, and cultural activities that are primarily intended for the GLBT community and its visibility. Most major cities in the United States sponsor pride groups, which are increasingly valued by marketers as ways to reach a broad cross-section of GLBT consumers.

- **National Lesbian & Gay Journalists Association** (NLGJA), *www.nlgja.org*

  The NLGJA is an organization of journalists, media professionals, educators, and students who work within the news industry to foster fair and accurate coverage of gay, lesbian, bisexual, and transgender issues. Since its founding in 1990, NLGJA has grown to a 1,300-member, 24-chapter organization in the United States with affiliations in Canada and Germany.

- **National Center for Lesbian Rights** (NCLR), *www.nclr.org*

  The NCLR sees itself as a national legal resource center with a primary commitment to advancing the rights and safety of lesbians and their families through a program of litigation, public policy advocacy, and public education.

- **Servicemembers Legal Defense Network** (SLDN), *www .sldn.org*

  This group emerged in 1993, shortly after the controversial "don't ask, don't tell" policy was adopted by the federal government. Under the policy, thousands of lesbian and gay service members realize their peril under military authority, and have relied on SLDN as their advocate and champion for fair treatment for all GLBT Americans who wish to serve their nation's military during war and in peacetime.

- **Gender Public Advocacy Coalition,** or GenderPAC, *www .gpac.org*

  The Gender Public Advocacy Coalition works to end discrimination and violence prompted by gender identification and stereotypes. This group has made tremendous strides in terms of public policy recognition and education about transgendered people; it also promotes understanding about the connection between all forms of discrimination based on gender stereotypes and sex, sexual orientation, age, race, and class.

- **Gay and Lesbian Victory Fund,** *www.victoryfund.org*

  While steeped in electoral politics and public service, the Gay and Lesbian Victory Fund's deepest commitment is to literally increasing the number of openly GLBT public officials at all levels of government leadership. The organization is entirely nonpartisan, and focuses on helping grow the skills and resources necessary for qualified GLBT candidates to gain public office throughout America, much as Emily's List has done for years on behalf of women leaders. Its 501(c)(3) arm is the Victory Institute, which provides professional skill building and offers full and partial scholarships to the executive programs at Harvard's Kennedy School of Government.

- **The Federation of Gay Games,** *www.gaygames.org*

  Founded in 1980 by former Olympian Dr. Tom Waddell, the organization fosters a quadrennial, global athletic and cultural event known as the Gay Games. In 2006, the Gay Games will be held in Chicago.

Its mission, above all, is to enhance the self-respect, understanding, and visibility of GLBT people throughout the world. While the federation itself does not host any games, like the International Olympic Committee, it breathes life into all gay sporting and cultural bodies. It is an important bridge for corporations and other groups to connect meaningfully with the active recreation and sport pursuits of the gay community, and through individual amateur sport federations that range from swimming, gymnastics, track and field, bowling, baseball, and many more. Sporting events have long been as popular with marketers as they are with gays and lesbians who are keen to excel in their athletic goals. A fundamental principle of the federation is that all activities be inclusive in nature and that no individual shall be excluded from participating on the basis of sexual orientation, gender, race, religion, nationality, ethnic origin, political beliefs, athletic/artistic ability, physical challenge, age, or health status.

- **Metropolitan Community Churches** (MCC), *www.mccchurch.org*

Founded in 1968 by an energetic Christian minister, Reverend Troy Perry, the global network of Metropolitan Community Churches today may be found in 22 nations worldwide, welcoming millions of GLBT worshippers and their families and friends. This Christian denomination today has grown to 43,000 members and adherents in almost 300 congregations.

During the past 36 years, MCC's work forever has changed the face of Christianity and helps fuel the international struggle for GLBT rights and equality among people of faith. (Similarly, there are several more special denominational groups in the Catholic, Jewish, and Protestant faiths that help in the struggle against bigotry and intolerance while encouraging GLBT people to worship in the religion of their choice or their family upbringing. The MCC movement appears to be among the very largest.)

- **Gay and Lesbian Association of Choruses, Inc.,** or GALA Choruses, *www.galachoruses.org*

  This is the world's only association supporting the GLBT choral movement. Its member choruses may be found in most major U.S. cities as well as in other nations, and represent over 10,000 singers and supporters who share a deep love of choral music and take pride in GLBT visibility and kinship. It aspires to the highest musical arts while generating understanding and visibility for proud openly gay artists and performers.

- **Gay and Lesbian Medical Association** (GLMA), *www.glma .org*

  Openly GLBT physicians and health care professionals are organized within GLMA as a professional society that also seeks to ensure equality in health care delivery for the community. This nonprofit is highly focused on public policy advocacy as well as professional skills growth, patient education, and the improvement and promotion of research to support improved health outcomes for GLBT households.

Appendix B

Commercial Closet Association
Best Practices

INTEGRATING GLBT SENSITIVITY
AND DIVERSITY INTO MAINSTREAM AND
BUSINESS-TO-BUSINESS ADVERTISING

Advertising seeks to sell, not offend. It may seem difficult today not to upset *someone*, but few minority groups are ridiculed as often and openly as gay, lesbian, bisexual, and transgender (GLBT) people.

We acknowledge that humor is an indispensable tool for creative professionals, yet while "political incorrectness" and irreverence may be assets to some in stand-up comedy, the goals of advertising are different—a laugh must also translate into sales from a wide variety of people. Over the years, hundreds of commercials have referred to GLBT people to spark attention and interest. Yet companies rarely consider what messages they may send inadvertently.

Although diversity and multicultural awareness are an increasing priority for corporations, and "sexual orientation" and "gender expression" concerns are addressed internally, these issues are often overlooked in general marketing communications. Advertising has not adapted to keep up with rapidly changing social attitudes of *consumers, businesses, investors, employees, vendors,* and *governments.*

The general population and media are increasingly aware of diversity and uncomfortable with messages lacking sensitivity. According to most recent public opinion surveys,

- at least 82 percent of Americans know someone gay;
- 81 percent of consumers don't care if products they regularly use are promoted to gays;
- 75 percent of youth support same-sex marriages;
- 54 percent of Americans support same-sex civil unions; and
- 42 percent of heterosexuals would be less likely to buy a product advertised on an antigay program.

Viacom/MTV launched 24-hour gay channel LOGO, prime-time TV featured up to 30 gay characters, the U.S. Supreme Court confirmed gay protections, and same-sex civil unions/domestic partner registries/marriage are legal in several states, Canada, and a number of European nations.

Big business increasingly protects its gay employees from discrimination (92.2 percent of Fortune 500 companies), offers equal benefits (43.2 percent of the Fortune 500), and explores gay marketing (36 percent of the Fortune 100), with $200–$250 million invested annually in U.S. gay media, events, and organizations.

Friends, family, and colleagues of GLBT people are very vocal, active, and sensitive allies to diversity issues, with national groups like PFLAG, GLSEN, and gay-straight alliances in schools.

GLBT people consistently self-identify in broad online surveys as much as 7 percent of the population (15 million-plus American adults). They belong to nearly every family and company and hold $641 billion in buying power in 2006, growing annually. They vary in race, age, religion, national origin, gender expression, ability, politics, profession, and class. About 1.2 million reported to the 2000 U.S. Census that they are partnered in rural areas, suburbs, and cities, appearing in 99 percent of counties nationwide, and one in five have children.

BEST PRACTICES

Because advertising is highly subjective, this is intended as a tool to assist executives in creating effective, inclusive mainstream and business-to-business advertising that is respectful of GLBT people, while promoting creativity, sales, and image goals.

Drawing on reporting observations, trial, and analysis from industry leaders, Commercial Closet Association recommends the following points (for actual advertising examples, please visit *www.commercialcloset.org*):

1. **Review the intent for including a same-sex come-on reference, GLBT storyline, or person, and avoid using them simply for a humorous punch line or an attention-getting stunt.** Are audiences intended to laugh at a same-sex "threat," the GLBT person, and/or sympathize with the negative response from a straight person?

2. **Be sensitive to GLBT stereotypes and avoid demeaning references to gay/lesbian sexual practice and derogatory language.** Advertising often stereotypes, but beware of complications. The effeminate gay man is an old idea that alienates many. Straight-male-fantasy "lipstick lesbians," duplicitous bisexuals, and deceitful/scary transgender people are narrow clichés that are polarizing.

3. **Be inclusive and diverse.** Whenever people are shown, integrate GLBT individuals/family members/friends/couples, reflecting varied ages, races, genders, etc. Language references to family, relationships, or gender should not be heterocentric.

4. **Avoid insults to masculinity or femininity.** GLBT people are frequently attacked in life for not meeting gender expectations.

5. **Do good research.** When conducting general research or forming new mainstream campaigns, GLBT perspectives should be considered and included as often as possible. Don't limit their input only to gay-targeted messages.

6. **Be consistent and confident.** Modifying or withdrawing ads suggests waffling and creates further trouble. Respond to criticism with business rationales, like diversity and the bottom line. Avoid time-restricted airings of commercials unless they legitimately deal with sexual situations inappropriate to youth.

EXECUTION OF BEST PRACTICES

1. Senior executives should visibly endorse and disseminate the Best Practices to all appropriate internal marketing and supporting ad agency staffs.
2. Because of GLBT diversity, focus groups are encouraged for guidance—avoid limiting to just one or two GLBT individuals. Tap into agencies and consultants with established gay-market expertise, as well as GLBT employee groups, for feedback and targeted efforts.
3. Incorporate GLBT inclusion into mainstream ad diversity representations. Integrate plans for targeted diversity marketing campaigns with gay and lesbian marketing.
4. Prepare consistent responses to media and consumer inquiries about the campaign.
5. Schedule professional, annual GLBT sensitivity training exclusively for ad and marketing staffs, and incorporate GLBT issues into general staff diversity trainings.

FACING CREATIVE CHALLENGES

Hundreds of companies and ad agencies represented in the Commercial Closet Ad Library have created GLBT-inclusive ads. They've done so to be edgy, to appeal to youth, for creative freshness, and to reflect the diversity of their customers. Here are some suggestions for creative challenges.

Gays and lesbians can be shown without relying on stereotypes or clichés. Try using:

- *Real gay or lesbian individuals.* Authenticity goes a long way.
- *Openly gay or lesbian celebrities or athletes*
- *Same-sex pairings in everyday situations,* such as at home, driving, shopping, or eating
- *Same-sex pairings with physical affection*
- *Sexuality reference through verbal, text, graphical, or anthropomorphic mentions*
- *Unexpected twists, countered time-worn clichés, and other humor sources*
- *Mix of masculine/feminine pairings for men or women as couples or friends:* butch-femme (men or women), femme-femme (men), butch-butch (women)

Bisexuals are rarely shown at all, but when they are it is usually as duplicitous cheaters. How do you avoid this characterization? Try using:

- *Depictions without a defined relationship to another person; ambiguous*
- *References through verbal, text, graphical, or anthropomorphic mentions*

Transgender is an umbrella term covering a range of gender expressions, identities, and situations: male-to-females/M2F, female-to-males/F2M, drag queens/camp, "bad drag," transsexuals, transvestites, and androgyny.

Trans people are not necessarily gay/lesbian. Most common in advertising are *male-to-females,* who typically show up as "deceptive" if they pass as women, or "frightening" if they do not. *"Bad drag"* and transvestites are intentionally unconvincing straight men half-dressed as women—for example, wearing wigs and mustaches simultaneously—as a joke or with a mock-subversive motive like spying. *Transvestites* are depicted in ads as heterosexual men "caught" cross-dressing in women's undergarments. *Drag queens* are portrayed as campy men impersonating women. *Transsexuals* have had a sex-change operation. *Female-to-males* and *androgyny*—ambiguous gender—are rarely depicted in advertising. Why not try:

- *Incorporate transgender people in everyday situations with acceptance as a twist, or employ camp/kitsch fun*
- *Use a real transgender person or real female impersonator for authenticity*
- *Depict female-to-male individuals, masculine/butch women, and "drag kings"*

A FINAL WORD ABOUT STEREOTYPES

Are stereotypes ever okay? It is often said that there is some truth to stereotypes, and indeed there are feminine/campy men, leather men, and masculine/sporty women in the GLBT community. It would be exclusionary to say they should never be depicted. Such characterizations may be used with caution if the intent is not to use GLBT stereotypes for ridicule and if their presence is more incidental or ultimately to counter the stereotypes.

WHY ADVERTISE? DOES IT WORK? WHAT ABOUT BACKLASH?

First, lots of companies already are doing it. Over 1,000 corporations and 500 ad agencies are represented in the Commercial Closet Ad Library, in categories such as alcohol/spirits, appliances, automotive, beauty, beverages, electronics, fashion, food, footwear, financial services, government, health care, media, package goods, restaurants, retail, soft drinks, telecommunications, travel, and more. Specific data is difficult to come by, as companies rarely share proprietary information. But many marketers have repeatedly incorporated GLBT themes into mainstream ads.

Second, diversity that includes "sexual orientation" is increasingly important to companies, consumers, investors, employees, vendors, and governments. Written policies and laws addressing the matter have become commonplace. They will expect it.

Third, consider your target audience. Is it really religious conservatives and the lowest common denominator, or everyday people? Across many age groups, from baby boomers to Generation X and Generation Y, a majority of the population is increasingly tolerant if not accepting of GLBT people. Don't forget that GLBT people are at least 7 percent of the population and represent $641 billion in buying power, and they all have family, friends, and colleagues who will act fiercely in their interest, too.

Fourth, GLBT themes and people in advertising reflect the true diversity of today's society and offer a creative freshness and twist to old storylines.

Fifth, Americans are more fair-minded, less interested in backlash. A 2004 Fleishman-Hillard/FH OutFront survey found eight out of ten American adults indicated that it did not matter to them if a company whose products they regularly use also promoted to the gay and lesbian community. Asked what they would do if boycotts were initiated against companies promoting themselves to gays and lesbians, 46 percent said "do nothing" and another 19 percent said they would "speak out against the boycott." Only 9 percent said they would participate in the boycott, while 21 percent would want to "learn more."

ABOUT COMMERCIAL CLOSET ASSOCIATION
(www.commercialcloset.org)

Commercial Closet is a nonprofit organization that educates advertisers, ad agencies, academics, the media, and consumers for more effective and informed references to lesbian, gay, bisexual and transgender people in advertising, creating a more accepting place for GLBT people in society. The organization provides tools, years of reporting on approaches that have and haven't worked, research, consumer feedback and input from marketing, advertising, media and education leaders, and an online library of over 3,000 global video and print GLBT-themed ad samples.

The project is led by a board of marketing, media and advertising professionals. Project founder and veteran advertising journalist Michael Wilke began covering gay marketing at its nascence over a decade ago. He has written extensively for Advertising Age, *along with* Adweek, *the* New York Times, *and* The Advocate, *and has appeared extensively on network TV.* (Revised April 2006)

Principle of Free Market Advertising Expression

Presented by the Commercial Closet Association and endorsed by the American Association of Advertising Agencies and the Association of National Advertisers, April 2006

America's bedrock commitment to entrepreneurialism and to free markets is older than our nation itself. Free markets recognize the worth of every single consumer without discrimination. In our extremely competitive economy, no company today can afford to neglect or shun any of its customers.

Corporate leaders today have advanced principles of inclusion and equal respect for all in their hiring and employment practices, as well as their advertising and selling strategies. The shameful times are behind us when some companies turned their backs on people because of the color of their skin, their ethnic origin, their physical disability or religious faith. Today, inclusion truly means everyone, including gays, lesbians, bisexual and transgender (GLBT) people.

Why? It is simply smart business for companies to market their products and services to every American. With $641 billion in buying power, GLBT households, along with millions of their family members and friends, play a critical role in the success of America's dynamic economy. They believe as we do that advertising their products respectfully to all customers helps their bottom line.

Although one-third of Fortune 500 companies and many others already have created inclusive marketing and advertising strategies, a handful of small groups have chosen to object to advertising that respects or targets gay and lesbian consumers.

These groups apply rigid agendas to boycott and target companies for merely doing what any business has the absolute right to do—reach out to all potential customers.

America's free enterprise system deserves much better. Together, we can and must speak up and be heard today—or choose to be silenced by a few. Therefore, we introduce these two simple sentences as a fundamental Principle of Free Market Advertising Expression. We ask fair-minded Americans and business leaders to join us in solidarity. All interested professional and civil rights associations that wish to endorse our Principle also are invited to do so.

CCA Principle of Free Market Advertising Expression

In America, all companies have the basic right to determine their own market expression—by advertising and selling to all customers respectfully and inclusively. We oppose all forms of bullying attacks intended to disrupt free commerce based on intolerance or hostility toward any consumers including gays and lesbians.